C'est Si Bon!

AT RISK CHILDREN
FOUNDATION, INC.

C'est Si Bon!

HAITIAN CUISINE COOKBOOK

AT-RISK
Children Foundation

Library of Congress Control Number: 2015901947
ISBN: Hardcover   978-1-5035-4126-9
               Softcover   978-1-5035-4127-6
               eBook   978-1-5035-4125-2

French and Creole Flavors Set Haiti Apart from Other Caribbean Islands

Print information available on the last page.

Rev. date: 10/09/2015

To order additional copies of this book, contact:
Xlibris
1-888-795-4274
www.Xlibris.com
Orders@Xlibris.com
604544

Contents

About ARCF 7

Acknowledgments 11

Introduction 13

History of Haitian Cuisine..15

The ARCF's Haitian Cuisine Cookbook 17

Appetizers 19

Entrées 42

Red Meat 54

Seafood 63

Vegetables...74

Gratiné 81

Soup du Jour 89

Salads...97

The Side Show...114

Sauces 120

In the Bread Basket..125

The Sweet Life: Desserts 135

Manje Kreyòl Haitian Créole Food...150

National Spirits and Liquors...152

Nonalcoholic Beverages 156

Index..159

ABOUT ARCF

At Risk Children Foundation (ARCF) is a nonprofit charitable organization with a 501(c)(3) status. Its mission is to provide educational opportunities, sustainability programs, and basic care to some of the neediest Haitian children. Our approach addresses the physical, social, spiritual, emotional, and educational needs of the children.

If you'd like to make a donation by check, please send your tax-deductible donation payable to

At Risk Children Foundation,
857 Bradley Street
West Hempstead, NY 11552

For online donation, please go to www.atriskchildren.org.

Thank you.

The idea for this book originated when Stephanie and Rose (ages sixteen and fifteen, respectively) made Paté kodé ak harran sour, a savory fried dough made with flour, herbs, garlic, and ground herring. It was delicious. Stephanie suggested that selling the fried dough with lemonade at fifteen gourdes apiece (US equivalent to forty cents) could raise money for school books. Stephanie's suggestion was one of the topics of our discussion at the July 2011 meeting, which set this entire project into motion!

Her idea resulted in the creation of C'est Si Bon "Haitian Cuisine Cookbook" by At Risk Children Foundation which you now hold in your hands.

These recipes of love support ARCF. The story is the children's, and the book is yours.

To make the paté kodé that Stephanie and Rose made in a large bowl, mix together these ingredients: all-purpose flour, water, chopped parsley, chopped shallot, chopped garlic, clove, seasoned ground herring, and a dash of hot pepper. Then fold everything together until made into a ball of dough. Form the dough into smaller two-inch balls and cook in a deep fryer or hot oil.

ACKNOWLEDGMENTS

This project would not have been possible without the dedication, support, and countless hours of creativity and input from Sergine Gaelle Altifor, Christiane Baptiste, Ryan Bishop, Edward V. Boria, Nina Boria, Deacon Norm Carroll, Daphnee Charlot, Marie G. Charlot, Tashima Charlot, Elizabeth Crowley, Kathleen Crowley, Robert E. Crowley, Anwar Farrell, Jean-Robert Fevry, Edith Jovin, Andrew Kernan, Harry Manigat, Lauretha Manigat, Claudy Mathurin, Endyne Mathurin, Mary Moran, and Glenna Stinson.

Thank you to all our wonderful friends, local Haitian food vendors, and Haitian restaurants for providing the fabulous recipes that helped make this book possible. Our deepest gratitude goes out to the many friends who contributed to the editing. A huge thank you to Charlene Chan of Chichilicous (ChichiLicious.com), Diane Gaillard of Pearl of Haiti Café (http://www.thepearloftheantilles.com), and Diana Pierre-Louis of The Real Haiti (www.therealhaiti.com) as well as to the other photographers who graciously contributed their beautiful photographs to our cookbook. We couldn't have done this without you.

We are enormously grateful to Elizabeth Crowley, Kathleen Crowley, Robert Crowley, and Anwar Farrell, who have generously helped us create the final product that is the *ARCF Haitian Cuisine Cookbook*. We shared our vision, and they made it a reality! Finally, a very special thank-you to the children who shared their recipes and the members who helped to create this cookbook.

The proceeds from this book and all donations will go to funding programs dedicated to assisting the orphans and vulnerable children in our care. These resources will be allocated to: (1) Chez Moi (My House) Phase II: expanding our capacity, which entails the construction of another building on the property; (2) upgrading the living conditions for our children in Custine, Cavaillon; (3) paying for the children to go to school; (4) building the Soveyo Library Learning Center; and (5) ensuring ARCF's long-term stability to care for disadvantaged Haitian children.

INTRODUCTION

This is a book about hope and the abundance life has to offer. This book is a symbol for people from all cultures around the world to reach out to the children in need who look to us for guidance and encouragement. It is about children overcoming destitution and striving to succeed. They want nothing that elicits pity or hopelessness in their difficult lives, but rather they are full of hope for a bright future. They need your investment to secure the productive and happy lives ahead of them.

This unique book is to be shared; please pass it along to as many people as possible, especially to friends, coworkers, and their families. Leave a copy wherever friends gather, your gym, your doctor's office, the teachers' lounge at your children's school. Take one to work and leave it in the break room. Send one to your niece in college and to your grandmother at the retirement home.

This project started from a staff meeting in Custine, Cavaillon, Haiti, following the idea of one child, and the response has been overwhelming. So many members and friends said this is just what they've been looking for and are ordering copies for themselves and others. Since its founding, ARCF has been supported solely by donations, members' donations, and religious bodies. No individual or entity has profited. Over 95 percent of every dollar donated is spent on mission-related services.

HISTORY OF
HAITIAN CUISINE

French and Creole Flavors Set Haiti Apart
from Other Caribbean Islands

The island of Hispaniola is home to the Dominican Republic and Haiti in the Caribbean. While the cuisine of the Dominican Republic is Spanish influenced, Haiti's fare is distinctly French and Creole, giving Haitian food a unique flavor among all Caribbean nations. This book incorporates this delicious fare in a way never before published.

Although the average Haitian's diet consists of mostly rice, corn, beans, yams, or millet, more extravagant fare is available, particularly in Pétion-Ville of the capital, Port-au-Prince, such as French cheeses, lobster, and frog legs. Tropical fruits native to the island include mango, coconut, guava, passion fruits, cerise, avocado, and pineapple. Popular beverages are made with these fresh fruits, and Juna, a local orange squash drink, is also well liked.

Haitian cuisine is different in several important ways from its regional counterparts. The main influence derives from French Creole and African cultures, with strong influence from native Taíno and Spanish culinary techniques. Although there are similarities to other cooking styles in the region, it carries characteristics known only to the country and appeals to the many visitors who frequent the island. Haitians cook using an extensive array of vegetables, meats, and spices. Peppers are often used to intensify flavor, so many dishes tend to be moderately spicy.

Rice, beans, and corn are staples in the Haitian diet, which are very filling because starches are high in carbohydrates. In rural areas, a popular dish such as *mais moulu* (mayi moulen), which is comparable to cornmeal, can be eaten with *sauce pois* (sos pwa)—a bean sauce made from one of many types of beans such as kidney, pinto, garbanzo beans, or pigeon peas. *Mais moulu* can be eaten with fish (often a red snapper) or alone, depending on personal preference. Tomato, oregano, cabbage, avocado, and red and green peppers are several of the many types of vegetables and fruits that are used in Haitian dishes. *Banane Pésée* (Bannan Pézé), flattened plantain slices that are fried in oil (known as tostones in the Dominican Republic and Puerto Rico), are eaten frequently in Haiti as both a snack food and as part of a meal. They are frequently eaten with *tassot* (deep-fried goat) and/or *griot* (deep-fried pork).

The ARCF's Haitian Cuisine Cookbook

The content of this book, the recipe portion, forms its heart. All these recipes were sent to us by members, families, and friends who want to help with our cause. This book represents an amazing collection of native Haitian staples and delicacies. Haitian food is both unique and tasty. Listed below are a multitude of recipes from which to choose. Some popular meat dishes include roast goat (*kabrit*), fried pork (*griot*), or poultry with a Creole sauce, *Poulet Creole*. Haiti also features a coastal cuisine consisting of local lobster, shrimp, and seafood. Local fruits including guava, pineapple, mango, banana, melons, and breadfruit are often used in fruit salads, compotes, and other delicious desserts. Coconuts are the number one choice of ingredient for use in beverages. Sugarcane makes a tasty snack and is commonly prepared and sold on streets to be enjoyed while one is out as well as at home. Many of the Haitian appetizers are lighter variations of main dishes, such as the boiled fish, conch (*lambi*), chicken (*poulet*), or fried pork (*griot*). Desserts will often include sweet and tasty fried bananas (*beyen*) or the traditional sweet potato bread (*pain patate*).

APPETIZERS

Whether you call them starters, one-bites, amuse-bouche, hors d'oeuvres, or *appetizers*, any type of tiny bite can be served before a meal in order to prepare the palate and excite the appetite.

Appetizers and hors d'oeuvres are the enticing entrance to a full meal. They pique the appetite without satisfying it and encourage easy conversation among gathered guests. Appetizers can be plated or passed, but they are most often finger food, easy to eat while standing and never overly messy in the hands.

You will notice that Haitians are, thankfully, not familiar with junk food, and their snacks are mostly considered light salads that can be eaten between meals, such as noni salad, papaya jam, or green papaya salad. Other snacks that can be found in the restaurants situated on the coast are fish and chicken croquettes and sweet Haitian vanilla bean marshmallows. Fries are also common but are not made of potatoes; Haitian fries include white fish fries and the famous breadfruit fries. Bananas, under any fresh or cooked form, are great snacks, especially because they are various, light, and accessible anywhere. Of course, commercial snacks are also available, such as crackers, roasted seeds, peanuts, and all other types of snacks you would expect to find in the United States.

Pimento Cheese

Pimento cheese is a well-known and beloved sandwich filling in Haiti as well as the Southern United States. A simple mixture of chopped cheddar cheese, mayonnaise, and pimentos, pimento cheese is great on crackers, baguette, or between two slices of crustless white bread.

Makes about three cups.

Ingredients

- 1 lb. sharp cheddar cheese, cut into cubes
- 1 (4 oz.) jar pimentos, drained and chopped
- 3 Tbsp. mayonnaise
- 2 cloves garlic, minced
- Salt and pepper to taste

Instructions

1. Place the cheese into a food processor and pulse until well chopped but not pureed.
2. Pour into a bowl and stir in the pimentos, mayonnaise, garlic, salt, and pepper.
3. To make sandwiches, spread between slices of white bread, cut off the crusts, and serve.

Variations

Try using a mixture of cheddar and Monterey Jack or softened cream cheese. Perk up the flavor with a dash of worcestershire, a touch of vinegar, a sprinkling of sugar, a dollop of mustard, or a drop of hot pepper sauce. Old-time recipes called for putting the cheese, garlic, and pimentos through a hand-cranked meat grinder. The resulting texture is incredible.

Mini Quiches

Ingredients

- 8 oz. cottage cheese, small curd
- 1/4 c. sour cream
- 4 oz. sharp cheddar cheese
- 1/2 c. buttermilk baking mix
- 1/4 c. melted butter
- 3 eggs

Instructions

1. Preheat oven to 350°F.
2. Mix all ingredients with an electric mixer.
3. Grease minimuffin tins and fill three-fourths full with egg mixture.
4. Bake for twenty minutes.

Avocados Stuffed with Crabmeat

The Scrumptious Pumpkin (thescrumptiouspumpkin.com)

Ingredients

- 1/2 lb. crab meat (fresh or canned)
- 3/4 c. celery, chopped
- 3 avocados, cut in half, seeded, and brushed with lime juice
- Mayonnaise to bind

Dressing

- 1 c. mayonnaise
- 1/2 c. sour cream
- 1/2 tsp. worcestershire sauce
- A few drops of Tabasco
- 1/4 tsp. rosemary, crushed
- 2 Tbsp. chili sauce or ketchup

Instructions

1. Mix shredded crabmeat with celery and just enough mayonnaise to bind.
2. In a separate bowl, mix the remaining ingredients to make the dressing.
3. Fill the center of the avocado halves with crabmeat filling.
4. Serve surrounded by lettuce leaves and topped with a dollop of mayonnaise or sour cream.

Taro Root Fritters
(Malanga Akra Beignets, "Taro Root")

Pearl of Haiti Café (www.thepearloftheantilles.com)

Ingredients

- ○ 1 lb. malanga, also called taro root or akra
- ○ 1 c. black-eyed peas (not dried)
- ○ 1 tsp. salt to taste
- ○ 1 tsp. black pepper to taste
- ○ 1 scallion
- ○ 1/2 onion, chopped
- ○ 1 garlic clove
- ○ 1/4 green bell pepper
- ○ 1 scotch bonnet pepper, seeded
- ○ 1 egg, beaten
- ○ 1 Tbsp. flour
- ○ 1/2 tsp. baking powder
- ○ 2 c. oil

Instructions

1. Grate the malanga to make two cups. In a food processor, mix the black-eyed peas, one-half cup water, salt, black pepper, scallion, onion, garlic, green bell pepper, and scotch bonnet pepper until it's well blended but still a thick consistency of the grated malanga.
2. In a bowl, mix the grated malanga with the black-eyed pea mixture. Mix in the beaten egg. Mix the flour and baking powder until you get a nice consistency.
3. Heat the oil on high heat until very hot. Drop mixture into oil in tablespoonful-size scoops.
4. Turn fritters when they reach a dark golden brown.
5. Scoop out any extra mix that breaks away from the batter in the hot oil so it does not clutter or burn the oil.
6. Drain on a paper towel.

Onion Tart
(Tarte a l'Oignon)

Ingredients

- 4 Tbsp. butter
- 5 onions, peeled and finely chopped
- 2 slices of ham, finely diced
- 1/2 tsp. salt
- 1/4 tsp. black pepper
- 1/2 tsp. sugar
- 4 Tbsp. plain flour
- 1/2 c. (125 ml.) milk
- 1/2 c. (125 ml.) heavy cream
- 4 eggs, beaten
- 4 ounces freshly grated Parmesan cheese

Instructions

1. Melt the butter in a pan; add the onions and cook over low heat for about eight minutes or until caramelized. Season with salt and pepper. Next, add the ham and sugar, and mix together.
2. Combine the milk and cream in a bowl. Set aside momentarily. Sprinkle the flour over the onion-and-ham mixture, and stir to blend. Stir in the milk mixture. Cook over medium heat until the mixture thickens. Remove from the heat and let cool for five to ten minutes.
3. Beat the eggs in a mixing bowl until light colored and frothy. Stir a spoonful of the onion mixture into the eggs to temper. Add another spoonful of the onion mixture and continue stirring. Repeat until all the onion-and-ham mixture has been stirred into the eggs and are thoroughly blended.

4. Stir in the grated Parmesan cheese. Next, pour the mixture into the prepared pie shell. Sprinkle with nutmeg.
5. Transfer to an oven preheated to 350°F (176°C) and bake for about thirty minutes or until the mixture has set and is lightly browned on top. Allow to cool for twenty minutes, then slice into wedges and serve with griots.

Chicken Patties
(Galettes de Poulet)

Filling

- 1 lb. ground chicken
- 1 medium onion, diced
- 3 garlic cloves, minced
- 1 medium shallot, diced
- 1 tsp. lime juice
- 1 tsp. adobo seasoning salt
- 1/2 scotch bonnet pepper, chopped
- 1/4 tsp. thyme
- 1/4 tsp. rosemary
- 1 Tbsp. tomato paste
- 2 tsp. olive oil

Dough

- o   2 c. of all-purpose flour
- o   1 tsp. salt
- o   1 c. water
- o   1 c. lard (manteca) or substitute with 1 c. of shortening and butter mixed together

Instructions

1. Combine salt water and flour in a large bowl. Mix well using your hands. Generously dust surface area. Knead until dough is firm and slightly sticky. Roll the pastry into a ball. Pack it up in a plastic wrap. Set aside for fifteen minutes.
2. Over medium heat, heat oil in a skillet or saucepan. Add onions, garlic, shallot, peppers, and seasoning mixture. Stir-fry for one minute until softened. Add the meat and simmer with water until meat is tender and water is absorbed. Add tomato paste and stir well until medium brown.
3. On a clean surface area, dust with flour generously to prevent dough from sticking. Using a rolling pin, flatten the dough and stretch into an oblong shape. Roll dough front to back and back to front until one-eighth inch thick. Spread the lard or shortening mix generously.
4. Fold in the flaps to cover over coated areas. Sprinkle the dough with flour, and roll out evenly. Form into a ball and set aside for fifteen minutes.
5. Repeat the steps to flatten and fold the dough. Wrap the dough ball in plastic and let refrigerate overnight.
6. Preheat oven to 375°F.
7. Bring out the dough, unwrap, and roll out evenly.
8. Divide dough into 2 1/2 inch disk-like shapes and roll disks of dough to 1/4 - 1/2 inch thick. Place dough disk in the palm of your hand and extend pieces with fingers. Place a tablespoonful of the filling on one side of the dough rounds. Fold and lightly press edges together with the tines of a fork.

9. Place the patties on a baking sheet. Brush the tops and edges of the patties with egg yolk before placing in the oven. Place a pan of water on the bottom rack of the oven.

10. Bake at 375°F for thirty minutes, then reduce heat to 300°F and bake for twenty minutes or until golden brown.

Beef Patties
(Galettes de Boeuf)

Ingredients

- 1 c. cold water
- 1 tsp. salt
- 3 c. all-purpose flour
- 1 c. vegetable shortening and 1/4 c. butter mixed together
- 1 egg yolk, beaten
- 2 tsp. of parsley
- 2 chopped shallots
- 1 chopped garlic clove
- 1 lb. ground beef, sautéed and seasoned
- 1 Tbsp. of beef broth
- Hot pepper to taste

Instructions

1. Pound the parsley, pepper, shallot, and garlic to a paste. Add paste and broth to cooked beef and mix well.
2. Cook covered on medium heat for ten minutes. Stir often.
3. Uncover until liquids are absorbed. Now, filling is ready.
4. Place flour in a large mixing bowl and make a hole in the center. Pour in water and salt. Mix lightly with a spoon without kneading. Place dough in refrigerator for thirty minutes.
5. Roll the dough into a rectangle one-fourth inch thick. Spread half the shortening/butter mix onto the dough. Fold one side over the middle and spread this section with the remaining shortening. Fold over the remaining section and again roll out to one-fourth-inch thickness. Fold again into thirds, and roll out. Repeat this rolling process a third time. Refrigerate dough overnight.

6. Roll the dough to about one-half-inch thickness. Cut the dough into 2 1/2 inch rounds.

7. Place a tablespoonful of beef filling on one side of the dough rounds. Fold and lightly press edges together with the tines of a fork. Place the patties on a baking sheet. Brush the tops and edges of the patties with egg yolk before placing in the oven. Place a pan of water on the bottom rack of the oven.

8. Bake at 400°F for thirty minutes, then reduce heat to 300°F and bake for twenty minutes or until golden brown.

Conch Fritters
(Beignets de Conque)

Diana Pierre-Louis of The Real Haiti (www.therealhaiti.com)

Ingredients

- 1 1/2 c. all-purpose flour
- 1 1/2 tsp. baking powder
- 1/4 c. finely chopped green bell pepper
- 1/4 c. finely chopped red pepper
- 1/2 small white onion, diced finely
- 1 garlic clove, minced
- 1 tbsp. finely chopped fresh parsley
- 1 Tbsp. finely chopped fresh thyme
- 1/2 scotch bonnet pepper, seeded and minced
- 1/4 c. milk
- 3/4 lb. chopped conch
- 1/4 tsp. salt (optional)
- 1/4 tsp. freshly ground black pepper

○   1 c. vegetable oil (for frying)

Instructions

1. In a food processor, combine all ingredients; process until blended.
2. Refrigerate the dressing until ready to serve.

Fritter

1. In a large bowl, mix flour and baking powder.
2. Add the bell peppers, onions, garlic, parsley, thyme, and scotch bonnet pepper.
3. Stir in milk; beat batter well. Stir in chopped conch, salt (if desired), and black pepper.
4. In deep skillet or electric fryer, heat oil to 375°F.
5. Using a slotted spoon, remove fritters; transfer to paper towels to drain.
6. Serve with the dressing in a separate bowl.

Kibbe

Baked kibbe is a traditional Lebanese dish that has been a constant in the Haitian family throughout the years. Considered by some as the national Lebanese dish, kibbe is a hearty meal or snack that anyone can enjoy. This traditional recipe can be served as an hors d'oeuvre or entrées. Let us show you the best way to make kibbe step by step through the Soveyo kibbe recipes so you can delight your friends and family.

Ingredients

- 1/2 c. bulgur wheat
- 1/2 c. chopped onion
- 1 garlic clove, minced
- 2 Tbsp. oil
- 1 lb. ground lamb (or beef)
- 3 Tbsp. pine nuts, lightly toasted
- 3/4 tsp. ground allspice
- 1/2 tsp. salt
- 1/3 c. chopped onion
- 1 1/2 tsp. salt
- 1 tsp. ground allspice
- 1/4 c. butter

Instructions

1. In a small bowl, soak bulgur in enough warm water to cover by one inch for one hour, and drain.

2. In a skillet, heat two tablespoons oil and add one-half cup chopped onion and garlic. Cook over medium heat for five minutes or until the onion is softened.

3. Add one-fourth of the ground lamb, pine nuts, three-fourth teaspoon allspice, and one-half teaspoon salt, and cook, stirring for five minutes or until lamb is no longer pink.

4. In a bowl, combine the remaining lamb, bulgur, one-third cup chopped onion, one-and-a-half teaspoon salt, and one teaspoon allspice.

5. Spread half of raw lamb in a buttered one-quart baking dish; cover with the cooked lamb and top with remaining raw lamb, smoothing the top.

6. Cook at 350°F for forty-five minutes.

Corn Fritters
(Beignets de Maïs)

Ingredients

- 1 can corn (1 oz.)
- Pinch of salt
- 1/2 c. flour
- 1 c. water
- 1/4 c. butter
- 3 eggs

Instructions

1. Mix flour, butter, salt, water, and three eggs.
2. Pour corn into batter, and mix well. Drop by tablespoons into very hot oil.
3. Brown; drain on paper towel. Serve with tomato sauce.

Fish Fritters
(Beignets de Poisson)

Ingredients

- o 1 egg yolk
- o 1 c. of cooked smoked herring or codfish
- o 2 egg whites
- o 1 Tbsp. salt
- o 2 scallions
- o 2 Tbsp. parsley
- o 1 tsp. lime juice
- o 1 tsp. hot sauce
- o 1 c. all-purpose flour
- o 1 Tbsp. baking powder
- o 2 1/2 c. water
- o 1/4 c. oil

Instructions

1. Combine salt, scallion, parsley, lime juice, and hot sauce, and set aside. Place flour with baking powder into a bowl.
2. Mix all the ingredients in the bowl and make a batter.
3. Pour the batter by spoonfuls into a pan of heated oil or deep fryer, and cook until golden brown on both sides.

Chicken Fritters
(Beignets dePoulet)

Ingredients

- 3 c. flour
- 1 c. water
- 1 tsp. finely chopped parsley
- 1 tsp. crushed hot pepper (Habanerachilies)
- 2 tsp. baking powder
- 1 c. chicken, cooked, boneless, and shredded
- 1 c. vegetable oil
- Salt to taste

Instructions

Combine flour with water. Add hot pepper, parsley, and baking powder. Let mixture rest for an hour. Add boneless, shredded chicken and salt. Heat oil, and drop in mixture by tablespoonfuls. Fry until golden brown, then serve hot.

ENTRÉES

Roti Chicken
(Poulet Roti)

Ingredients

- 3 tbsp. - 4 tbsp. butter, softened
- 1 garlic clove, peeled
- 1/4 tsp. ground hot red pepper
- 1 c. soft, fresh bread crumbs
- 1 1/2 tsp. salt
- 4 Tbsp. lime juice
- 1/4 tsp. ground nutmeg
- 1 Tbsp. finely grated lime rind
- 1/2 tsp. salt
- 1 c. chicken stock, fresh or canned
- 3 medium-size ripe bananas
- 1 tsp. dark brown sugar *ing*
- 3 1/2–4 lbs. whole roasted chicken
- Freshly ground black pepper to taste

Instructions

1. Preheat the oven to 350°F.
2. In a heavy six-inch to eight-inch skillet, melt three tablespoons of butter over moderate heat.
3. When the foam begins to subside, drop in the garlic and stir for ten to fifteen seconds.
4. Remove and discard the garlic; add the bread crumbs and stir until they are crisp and brown.
5. Turn off the heat, stir in three tablespoons of the lime juice, lime rind, brown sugar, nutmeg, red pepper, one teaspoon of the salt, and pepper to taste.
6. Set this bread-crumb stuffing aside.
7. Peel and chop bananas finely, and put them into a small bowl.

8. Add the remaining tablespoons of lime juice, the remaining one-half teaspoon of salt, and pepper to taste to the chopped bananas, and toss the ingredients with a spoon to combine this banana stuffing thoroughly.

9. Pat the chicken completely dry inside and out with paper towels.

10. Fill the breast cavity with the banana stuffing, and close the opening by lacing it with skewers or sewing it with a large needle and heavy white thread.

11. Fill the smaller neck cavity with the bread-crumb stuffing, and skewer or sew the opening shut.

12. Truss the chicken securely, and with a pastry brush, coat it thoroughly with the four tablespoons of softened butter.

13. Place the bird on a rack in a shallow roasting pan just large enough to hold it comfortably, and roast in the middle of the oven for about 1 1/2 hours, basting occasionally with the juices as they accumulate in the pan.

14. To test for doneness, pierce the thigh of the bird with the point of a small sharp knife.

15. The juice that trickles out should be pale yellow; if it is tinged with pink, roast the chicken for another five to ten minutes.

16. Transfer the bird to a large heated platter, cut off and discard the trussing strings, and let the chicken rest for about five minutes for easier carving.

17. Meanwhile, skim the fat from the juices in the pan, and pour in the cup of stock.

18. Bring to a boil over high heat, stirring to the bottom of the pan.

19. Cook the sauce briskly for two or three minutes, taste for seasoning, and pour into a small bowl.

Chicken in Sauce
(Poulet en Sauce)

Diana Pierre-Louis of The Real Haiti (www.therealhaiti.com)

Ingredients

- 1 medium-size frying chicken
- 1 large onion, sliced in rounds
- 1 large pepper (mild or hot, depending on your taste)
- several cloves of garlic, mashed or minced
- 3/4 c. of tomato sauce
- 3 Tbsp. sugar
- Generous pinch of salt
- Lime or lemon
- Dash of oil

Instructions

1. Preheat oven to 375°F.
2. Wash chicken well and cut into pieces. Rub each piece with the lemon or lime and sprinkle with salt.

3. Heat oil in a heavy pan (cast-iron is best as the pan will then be placed in the oven).
4. Fry the chicken pieces in hot oil.
5. While chicken is frying, combine the garlic, sugar, tomato sauce, and salt in a bowl. Mix well.
6. After a few minutes, add the onion rounds and pepper rounds to the pan with the chicken. Stir well.
7. Within a few minutes, the chicken should be well browned. Remove from heat, drain off excess oil, and add the tomato mixture to the pan. Stir well.
8. Place the entire pan in the oven and bake uncovered for twenty minutes or until the chicken is cooked completely.
9. Transfer cooked chicken and sauce to a platter, and garnish with rounds of raw onion and a pile of pickles.
10. Ketchup can be substituted for the tomato sauce if sugar is omitted. Tomato paste can be substituted for the sauce. Use one-half cup minus one tablespoon of paste. Add three tablespoons of water to the tomato mixture.
11. This dish goes well with dire blan (plain white rice)—placing the chicken on top of the rice, the sauce can then be poured over the top. Finish by garnishing with raw onion and pickles.

Use part can of plum tomatos instead of paste, etc → for tomato averse

Turkey in Sauce
(Dinde en Sauce)

Ingredients

- 8 cloves garlic, peeled
- Salt to taste
- 8 sprigs flat-leaf parsley
- 8 sprigs thyme
- (2 sprigs oregano)
- 1 c. fresh lemon juice
- 2 Tbsp. apple cider vinegar
- 20 lbs. brined or kosher turkey, trimmed of excess fat and skin and rinsed, neck and giblets reserved
- 6 limes, halved
- 2 Tbsp. adobo
- Freshly ground black pepper
- 1/3 c. ham, finely chopped , chicken bacon
- 2 Scotch bonnet peppers, diced
- 8 sweet small Cachucha peppers or ajicitos dulces *or* 1 large Cubanelle pepper, seeded and cut into 1/3 inch dice
- 1/2 c. red onion, finely chopped
- 1/4 c. manzanilla olives with pimento, finely chopped
- 20 capers, finely chopped

- o 1 bottle dry red wine
- o 1 tsp. ground achiote
- o 6 oz. tomato paste
- o 2 Tbsp. extra virgin olive oil
- o 2 c. chicken stock or broth
- o 1/2 red onion, peeled and thinly sliced
- o 1/2 red bell pepper, thinly sliced

Instructions

1. To prepare for marinating the turkey, use a large mortar and pestle or small food processor to mash or purée garlic with a pinch of salt, five sprigs of parsley, five sprigs of thyme, and oregano. Transfer to bowl. Add lemon juice, one tablespoon vinegar, and two teaspoons water. Set aside.
2. With long paring knife, make slits 1/2 inch to 1 1/2 inches deep about 1/2 inch apart all over the turkey, including the legs and the wings. Widen slits with fingers or spoon.
3. Rub limes over the turkey, squeezing out juice and massaging into the meat. Discard halves and excess juice.
4. Sprinkle turkey all over with adobo, and season with salt and black pepper to taste.
5. Strain the garlic-herb purée, reserving the liquid. Place purée in a mixing bowl, and add chopped ham, Scotch bonnet peppers, sweet peppers, chopped onion, olives, and capers. Mix well.
6. To protect hands from being irritated while handling the hot pepper mixture, wear thin latex or rubber gloves.
7. Press large pinches of the hot pepper mixture into the turkey slits. If any mixture remains after holes are filled, place it in the cavity along with the reserved neck and giblets.
8. Place turkey in deep nonreactive pot and pour reserved juice from garlic purée on top, massaging it in well. Pour wine over the turkey, cover, and refrigerate overnight.
9. To prepare for roasting the turkey, set oven rack low. Heat oven to 375°F.

10. Reserve three cups of wine liquid and set aside. Discard the rest.
11. Into wine, stir achiote, tomato paste, remaining tablespoons of vinegar, olive oil, and chicken stock.
12. Place turkey in roasting pan along with sliced onion and red bell pepper and remaining parsley and thyme. Pour half the wine mixture over the turkey. Reserve rest for basting.
13. Begin roasting turkey breast side up, basting every fifteen minutes. Every thirty minutes for the first two hours, flip turkey, first breast side down, then breast up.
14. After the first two hours, leave breast side up and continue roasting and basting for sixty to ninety minutes longer. (Turkey is done when the thickest part of the breast registers at 160°F on meat thermometer and thickest part of thigh registers 165°F.)
15. Remove from oven; cover it with foil, and let it rest for twenty minutes before carving.
16. Strain pan juices into small saucepan, skim off and discard fat, and serve drippings as gravy.

Chicken Creole
(Poulet Créole)

Ingredients

- 1 large onion, chopped (1 c.)
- 1/2 tsp. salt
- 3/4 c. green pepper (1 medium) diced
- 2 c. cubed cooked chicken
- 1 large clove of garlic, crushed
- 1/4 tsp. sugar
- 3 tbsp. oil
- Freshly ground pepper
- 2 Tbsp. flour
- Hot cooked rice
- 1 can (6 oz.) tomato paste
- 2 1/4 c. chicken broth
- 1/4 tsp. hot pepper sauce

Instructions

1. In a large skillet, sauté onion, green pepper, and garlic in oil until tender, stirring occasionally. Add flour; cook and stir just until flour starts to brown.
2. Stir in tomato paste, broth, salt, sugar, and pepper sauce.
3. Cook and stir until mixture comes to boil and thickens.
4. Simmer uncovered for five minutes, stirring occasionally.
5. Stir in chicken and season with freshly ground pepper.
6. Heat until hot.
7. Serve over hot rice.

Roast Duck with Orange Sauce
(Canard Rôti avec Sauce à L'orange)

Canard, or *caneton*, *à l'orange* can seem intimidating, but it's actually quite easy to prepare. If you can roast a chicken, you can roast a duck. The trickiest part of the sauce is caramelizing the sugar. Just take care not to leave the saucepan over heat too long, and you should have no problem. Great for dinner parties.

Makes four to six servings.

Ingredients

- 1 whole duck (5 lbs.)
- Salt and pepper to season
- 3 oranges
- 1/4 c. sugar
- 3 Tbsp. red wine vinegar
- 2 c. duck or chicken stock
- 1/3 c. white wine or port
- 2 Tbsp. cornstarch or arrowroot
- 3 Tbsp. Grand Marnier liqueur
- 2 Tbsp. butter, softened

Method

1. Preheat oven to 425°F. Remove the duck from the refrigerator about thirty minutes before you put it in the oven, and let it come to room temperature. Wash the duck with cold water, pat it dry with paper towels, and tuck the wings under the body to keep them from burning. Prick the duck skin all over with a skewer or toothpick. Trim any excess fat from the opening of the body cavity. Season the duck liberally inside and outside with salt and pepper.

2. Set the duck on a rack in a roasting pan. Place the roasting pan in the lowest rack of the oven and roast for about fifteen minutes. Then reduce the heat to 350°F and continue to roast, basting with the pan juices every fifteen to twenty minutes until the duck is cooked through and the temperature in the thickest part of the thigh measures between 165°F and 175°F (use a meat thermometer). Depending on your oven and the size of your bird, this should take anywhere from 1 to 1 1/2 hours.

3. While your duck is roasting, prepare the sauce. Zest the oranges, taking care not to get any of the bitter white pith. Squeeze the juice from the oranges, and set the zest and juice aside.

4. Add the sugar and vinegar to a medium-size saucepan. Set the saucepan over medium-low heat and cook, stirring constantly, until the sugar is completely dissolved and starts to turn golden brown. Immediately remove from heat and carefully stir in the reserved orange juice (the caramelized sugar will splatter).

5. Return to the flame and add the chicken stock. Whisk over low heat until the caramelized sugar is completely dissolved. At this point, the sauce base can be set aside until the duck is finished roasting.

6. When the duck is finished, remove it from the oven, tent it loosely with foil, and set it aside to rest for fifteen to twenty minutes. Skim any excess fat from the roasting pan and add the wine or port. Place the roasting pan on the stovetop over medium flame, and bring the wine and pan juices to a boil,

scraping up any bits of drippings off the pan. Pour the pan juices into the saucepan with the sauce base. Strain the sauce, return it to the saucepan, and stir in the reserved orange zest.

7. Bring the sauce to a simmer over low heat. Stir the cornstarch and Grand Marnier together in a small bowl, then whisk the slurry into the simmering sauce to thicken it. Remove the sauce from heat, and slowly whisk in the butter to enrich the sauce.

8. Carve the duck and place it on a serving platter. Serve the sauce in a sauceboat alongside the carved roast duck.

Variations

○ A platter of *canard à l'orange* is often garnished with peeled orange segments.
○ A tablespoon of red currant preserves is sometimes stirred into the sauce at the end.

RED MEAT

Fried Cubed Beef or Goat

(Tassot au Bouef—Cabrit)

Ingredients

- 2 lb. steak or goat cut into small cubes
- 1/2 c. of chopped shallots
- 1/2 c. of orange juice
- 1/4 c. lime or lemon juice
- 1/2 c. of vegetable oil
- Salt and pepper to taste
- 1 tsp. of parsley

Instructions

1. Put all ingredients except the oil in a large pot and marinate for at least four hours.

2. Transfer meat mixture to a medium saucepan or pressure cooker, and add water to cover.
3. Heat to a boil and reduce heat. Simmer covered until meat is very tender.
4. Fry meat in a large pan until crisp and golden brown.

Seasoned Beef Meatballs

(Boulettes de Boeuf Assaisonné)

Ingredients

- 1 lb. freshly ground beef
- 1 egg
- 2 tsp. salt
- 1/4 tsp. black pepper
- 1 small minced onion
- 1 tsp. parsley
- 1/2 tsp. oregano
- 2 garlic cloves
- 4 slices bread (edges trimmed)
- 1/2 c. flour
- 1/2 c. oil

Instructions

1. Mix ground beef, egg, salt, black pepper, onion, spices, and garlic.
2. Soak bread in one tablespoon water and mix with meat.
3. Roll into golf-ball-size meatballs and dip in flour.
4. Pan fry in oil until golden brown.
5. Drain on paper towel.

Beef Stew
(Ragoût de Boeuf)

This simple, flavorful dish is characteristic of the Haitian love of tasty meat and vegetable dishes using tomatoes and peppers. *Beef à l'haïtienne* tastes even better if served the next day. Makes four to six servings.

Ingredients

- 1 lb. beef shoulder or chuck roast, cubed
- 2 tsp. salt
- Water to cover
- 1/4 c. oil
- 1 onion, thinly sliced
- 1 carrot, sliced
- 2 red or green peppers, chopped
- 2–4 garlic cloves, minced
- 1–4 hot chili pepper, minced
- 2 c. tomatoes, seeded and chopped
- 1 Tbsp. red wine vinegar
- Salt and pepper to taste

Instructions

1. Place the beef and salt in a large pot, and add enough water just to cover the meat. Bring to a boil over high heat, and then reduce heat to low and simmer uncovered until the beef is tender and the water is almost completely evaporated, forty-five minutes to an hour.
2. While the beef is simmering, heat the oil in a skillet over medium flame. Add the carrots, onion, peppers, garlic, and chili peppers and sauté until the onions and peppers are wilted.

3. Add the tomatoes, vinegar, salt, and pepper. Reduce heat to low and simmer until almost all liquid is evaporated, twenty to twenty-five minutes.

4. Stir the beef into the onions and peppers and simmer for another twenty to thirty minutes, adding a little water if necessary. Adjust seasoning to taste and serve with rice.

5. This dish can be made fiery hot or very mild, depending on the number of chilies you add.

Fried Pork
(Porc Frit Griots)

Charlene Chan of Chichilicious (ChichiLicious.com)

This rich, flavorful dish is one of Haiti's most popular and is invariably served at parties and family gatherings. Cubes of pork are soaked in a sour orange marinade and then slow-roasted until tender. The tender morsels are then given a final fry in oil until delectably caramelized. Usually served with fried plantain.

Ingredients

- 3 lbs. shoulder of pork, cut into 1 to 2 inch cubes
- 1/2 c. of chopped shallots
- 1 c. of bitter orange juice
- 1/2 c. of vegetable oil
- Salt, pepper, and hot pepper to taste
- 1 tsp. thyme
- 1 large onion chopped

Instructions

1. Put all ingredients except the oil in a large pot and marinate overnight in the refrigerator.
2. Place the marinated pork on the stove, add water to cover all ingredients, and boil on medium heat for forty-five minutes.
3. Once cooked, drain the mixture, add oil, and fry the pork in the pot until brown and crusty on the outside but tender on the inside. As another option, bake in the oven in a large baking pan until tender.

Excellent served with pikliz.

SEAFOOD

Stewed Conch
(Lambi en Sauce)

Ingredients

- 1 (0.5 lb.) box of conch (lambi)
- 1 lime
- 1 sour orange
- 1 tsp. garlic powder
- 1 tsp. thyme
- 1 tsp. black pepper
- 1 hot pepper
- 1 onion
- Shallots
- 1 can tomato paste

Instructions

1. Using a meat mallet, pound the conch until tenderized.
2. Clean the meat thoroughly with the lime and/or sour orange juice.
3. Season well. For best results, keep refrigerated overnight.
4. Bring six cups of water to a boil using a pressure cooker.
5. Place the meat into the cooker.
6. Close cover securely with regulator in place.
7. Cook for an hour. Let cool.
8. Heat olive oil in a frying pan, and brown meat for ten minutes.
9. Set aside the meat, and prepare the sauce.
10. Sauté the onions and shallots.
11. Stir in tomato paste and add the browned conch.
12. Serve hot and enjoy!

Steamed Fish
(Poisson Cuit à la Vapeur)

Ingredients

- 2 lb. fish, cleaned (typically salmon, red snapper, mackerel, or catfish, but any type of fish can be used)
- 3 c. water
- 2 limes, *peeled + zest.*
- 1/2 c. scallions
- 1 medium onion, chopped
- 1/2 c. carrots, diced
- 1 clove of garlic, minced
- 3 Tbsp. tomato paste
- 1 tsp. parsley
- 1 tsp. thyme
- Salt, black pepper, and hot pepper to taste

Instructions

1. Boil water in a large pot, and then combine all ingredients excluding the fish.
2. Cook for ten minutes then add the fish.
3. Simmer until fish is flaky, about ten minutes.

Marinated Red Snapper

(Red Snapper Mariné)

Ingredients

- 1 medium snapper
- 3 limes (or lemons)
- 1/2 tsp. sea salt
- Pepper to taste
- 1/4 tsp. each, thyme and parsley
- Juice from one fresh lemon or lime
- Fresh crushed garlic cloves
- 1 hot pepper, sliced into strips
- 1 sweet pepper, sliced into strips
- 1 onion, sliced
- 1/4 c. oil
- 1–2 c. water

Instructions

1. Clean the fish with water, rub with the juice of one lime, and rinse again and place in a shallow pan.
2. Mix all spices, garlic, onion, and peppers together with the juice from remaining limes. Pour over fish; let fish marinate for about one hour. Drain marinade off and reserve for later.
3. In a sauté pan, pour half a cup of oil; when oil is hot, add the snapper. Cook over medium heat for five minutes.
4. Add marinade to pan with the water; let simmer for fifteen to twenty minutes or until fish is tender. If needed, season with additional spices such as red pepper, parsley, or salt to taste.

Creole Lobster
(Homard Creole)

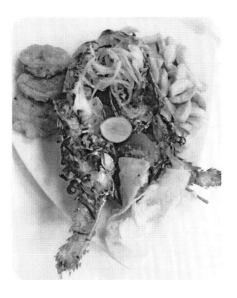

Diana Pierre-Louis of The Real Haiti (www.therealhaiti.com)

Ingredients

- 4 oz. chopped fresh spinach
- 1 1/4 c. prepared mayonnaise
- 3 anchovy fillets, minced
- 2 small cloves of garlic, minced
- 1 1/2 tsp. minced chives
- 1 tsp. minced parsley
- 1 tsp. capers
- 1/2 tsp. fresh lemon juice
- 1/4 tsp. salt
- 1/4 tsp. pepper

Lobster

- Vegetable oil for frying
- 1 c. dry breadcrumbs
- 1/4 c. ground almonds
- 1 1/2 Tbsp. chopped chives
- 8 (4 oz.) lobster tails, shells discarded
- 1 c. prepared mayonnaise

Sauce

1. Stir together spinach, mayonnaise, anchovy, garlic, chives, parsley, capers, salt, and pepper in a small bowl until well blended. Cover and refrigerate overnight. Let stand for one hour at room temperature before serving.

Lobster

1. Heat oil to 350°F degrees in a fryer or deep pan.
2. Stir together breadcrumbs, almonds, and chives in a pie plate.
3. Coat lobster tails with mayonnaise, wiping off excess, and then in breadcrumb mixture.
4. Fry about five minutes until golden brown on all sides. Drain well on paper towels. Serve with sauce.

Recipe by Restaurant Ti-Marché.

ShrimpCreole
(Crevettes à la Créole)

Ingredients

- o 1 lb. shrimp, cleaned and cooked
- o 1/4 c. chopped green pepper
- o 1/2 c. chopped onion
- o 1 clove of garlic, minced
- o 3 Tbsp. butter
- o 2 c. canned tomatoes
- o 1 (8 oz.) can tomato sauce
- o 1/2 c. water
- o 1 c. finely chopped celery
- o 1 tsp. prepared mustard
- o 1/2 tsp. sugar
- o Dash of Tabasco sauce
- o 1 tsp. salt
- o 1/8 tsp. pepper
- o 1 bay leaf
- o 3 c. hot cooked rice

Instructions

1. Sauté pepper, onion, celery, and garlic in butter. Add tomatoes, tomato sauce, water, prepared mustard, sugar, Tabasco, seasonings, and bay leaf.
2. Simmer twenty to twenty-five minutes, stirring often.
3. Add shrimp and simmer for ten minutes longer. Remove bay leaf.
4. Serve over rice.

By Restaurant Ti-Marché

Grilled Salmon
(Saumon Grillé)

Ingredient

- 3 lbs. fresh salmon steaks
- 1/4 c. lemon juice
- 1/4 c. white wine
- 1 Tbsp. melted butter
- 1/2 c. Vidalia onion dressing
- Medium red onion, sliced
- Red bell pepper, julienned
- Ground black pepper to taste

Instructions

1. Place salmon steaks in a large bowl, and pour lemon juice over them. Clean salmon thoroughly and rinse in cold water.
2. Place clean salmon in an ovenproof dish. Add wine, Vidalia onion dressing, and black pepper. Mix well and refrigerate for one-half hour.

3. Pour one-half of melted butter on salmon steaks.
4. Bake in preheated 375°F oven for twenty minutes or until golden brown. Turn them over and pour remaining butter on them; bake until golden brown. Add onion and red bell pepper, and mix.

VEGETABLES

Mixed Vegetable Stew
(Ragoût de Légumes Mélangés)

Ingredients

- 2 lbs. beef to stew
- 1/4 - 1/2 c. of vegetable oil
- 1 green bell pepper
- 1 head of cabbage
- 2 cans or boxes of frozen lima beans
- 1/2 - 1 bag of frozen green beans (medium-size bag)
- 2–3 peeled and sliced carrots
- 1 box frozen spinach
- 2 Tbsp. butter
- 2–3 cubes chicken bouillon
- 1/2 c. tomato paste

Instructions

1. You want to first brown the beef with a small amount of oil.
2. Then add tomato paste and mix in enough water to cover the beef.
3. Cut up some green bell pepper in large pieces and place on top of the beef while it is cooking.
4. Let the beef cook until tender, continually adding tomato paste mixture as needed so the beef does not burn or dry out.
5. Once beef is tender, in another pot, place a small amount of water, and cut the cabbage in large slices and place in the water.
6. Add the lima and green beans and carrots; cover and let steam.
7. Once veggies are somewhat tender, add the spinach and pour a small amount of the oil over the veggies.

8. Add the butter and one cube of bouillon. Continue to let steam.
9. Once tender, add veggies to the beef mixture; stir everything together and let cook for about twenty minutes.
10. If more seasoning is needed, add another bouillon cube.

This goes great with white rice and black beans that have been cooked down and blended in a blender to make sauce pois (recipe on page 114).

Variations

Of course, there are many ways to prepare legume, and several recipes are provided here. We thought this was the easiest recipe to start with.

The really important thing in preparing any meat dish is the way you clean and prepare the meat before cooking. You should wash the beef with salt, lime, and water. You can also use some vinegar. Rinse the meat after cleaning, and marinate it in a blended paste of green bell pepper, green onion, parsley, and vinegar. You can also add garlic to the paste if you like. Rub the paste on the meat and let marinate. After the meat has marinated, just drop it in the pot as I first discussed in the beginning of the recipe. As with any recipe, it takes practice and variations to get it just right. Good luck and let us know how it turned out!

Eggplant Mixed and Watercress
(Aubergines mixte et cresson)

Ingredients

- 2 lbs. round steaks, trimmed of all fat and cut into 2-inch cubes
- 1/4 - 1/2 c. vegetable oil
- Eggplant, chopped into 2-inch cubes
- Chayote (militon)
- Green bell peppers, chopped into 2-inch pieces
- Scallions, chopped finely
- 2 garlic cloves, minced
- Fresh parsley, chopped
- 1 large head of cabbage, outer leaves and core removed and chopped into 2-inch pieces
- 20 oz. Fordhook Lima Beans
- 12 oz. frozen string beans, chopped into 2-inch pieces
- 2–3 carrots, peeled and sliced into 2-inch pieces
- 1 (10 oz.) box-frozen chopped spinach
- Bunch watercress, chopped
- 4–5 cubes chicken bouillon
- 1/2 - 3/4 c. tomato paste
- 2–3 Tbsp. lemon juice
- Salt and freshly ground black pepper to taste
- Garlic powder to taste
- Pickles
- Seasoning powder (adobo seasoning)

Instructions

1. Wash beef with lemon juice and salt; allow to marinate for ten minutes. Rinse with cold water.
2. Make a paste from green pepper, green onions, parsley, garlic, and vinegar; rub it into meat and let marinate for about thirty minutes.
3. Brown beef in small amount of oil. Add tomato paste, seasonings, and water to cover the beef. Add chopped green bell pepper and place on top of the beef while it is cooking. Let the beef cook until tender, continually adding tomato paste mixture as needed so beef does not burn or dry out.
4. After meat is tender, bring a large pot with a medium amount of water to a boil, and start placing in the vegetables. First, add the cabbage and eggplant; next, add the lima beans and green beans. Add the carrots and chayote—allow to steam until somewhat tender, and then add spinach and watercress.
5. Pour some oil over the vegetables; add the butter and one bouillon cube. Continue to let steam till tender.
6. Once tender, add the vegetables to beef mixture, and stir everything together.
7. Let cook for another ten to twenty minutes, and add seasoning as needed.

This goes very well with white rice and black beans or kidney beans that have been cooked down and blended in a blender to make sauce pois (recipe on page 114). Enjoy!

Eggplant Parmesan

(Aubergine au Parmesan)

Ingredients

- 1 medium eggplant
- 2 green peppers, chopped
- 1 c. bread crumbs
- 2 onions, chopped
- 1/2 c. Parmesan cheese
- 1/4 tsp. thyme
- 2 Tbsp. chopped parsley
- 2 Tbsp. oil
- 1 tsp. salt
- 1 tsp. oregano
- 1/8 tsp. pepper
- 3 Tbsp. tomato paste
- 1 clove of garlic, minced
- 1 to 2 c. grated swiss cheese
- 4 tomatoes, chopped
- 1/4 c. additional Parmesan

Instructions

1. Preheat oven to 375°F degrees.
2. Cut eggplant into one-half-inch slices.
3. Cover eggplant completely with hot water and let stand for five minutes. Dry slices.
4. Fry in one-third cup of oil until lightly browned on each side.
5. Put in bottom of nine-by-thirteen-inch baking pan or casserole dish.
6. Combine next seven ingredients in a blender and blend well.
7. Sprinkle mixture over the eggplant.

8. In a saucepan, combine tomatoes, green peppers, onions, oil, garlic, and tomato paste and let simmer uncovered for about twenty minutes.
9. Spread on top of crumb mixture and eggplant.
10. Top with swiss cheese and the rest of the Parmesan cheese.
11. Bake for ten to fifteen minutes. Can be made ahead, refrigerated, and baked when ready to use.

GRATINÉ

Macaroni Gratiné
(Macaroni au Gratin)

Ingredients

- 16 oz. package of macaroni
- 1 whole onion, diced
- 8 oz. cooked ziti (or any pasta of choice)
- Onion, green or red peppers (optional)
- 2 chicken bouillon cubes
- 2/3 Velveeta cheese block, cut into small cubes
- 2 (12 oz.) cans of evaporated milk
- 1/2 c. of butter
- 1/2 c. of mayonnaise
- 1 c. of Parmesan cheese
- Salt (optional)

Instructions

1. Preheat oven at 300°F degrees.
2. Bring a large pot of water to boil over high heat.
3. Add the macaroni, and let it cook until soft but firm.

4. Add the diced onions and bouillon, reduce heat, and stir occasionally.
5. Stir in the Velveeta cheese until completely melted.
6. Keep stirring constantly to avoid the cheese from sticking to the bottom.
7. Add butter, mayonnaise, and Parmesan cheese.
8. Pour in the evaporated milk, and stir.
9. Turn heat off, and pour mixture into greased baking sheet or casserole dish.
10. Bake for fifteen minutes or until slightly browned, checking every five minutes.

Potato Gratiné
(Pomme de Terre Gratiné)

Ingredients

- 2 lb. Yukon Gold or russet potatoes, peeled
- 3 c. whipped or heavy cream
- 1 tsp. kosher salt
- 1/8 tsp. freshly ground black pepper
- Generous pinch of freshly grated nutmeg
- 2 cloves garlic, peeled and smashed
- 3/4 c. finely shredded gruyère, Emmentaler, or Comté

Instructions

1. Heat the oven to 400°F. Carefully cut the potatoes into one-eighth-inch slices (no thicker).
2. Put the potatoes in a large heavy-based saucepan, and add the cream, salt, pepper, nutmeg, and garlic. Cook the mixture over medium-high heat until the cream is boiling, stirring occasionally (very gently with a rubber spatula so you don't break up the slices).

3. When the cream boils, pour the mixture into a two-and-a-half- or three-quart baking dish. If you don't want a tender but garlicky surprise mouthful, remove and discard the garlic cloves. Shake the dish a bit to let the slices settle, and then sprinkle the surface with the cheese.

4. Bake in the hot oven until the top is deep golden brown, the cream has thickened, and the potatoes are extremely tender when pierced with a knife, about forty minutes. Don't worry if the dish looks too watery at this point; it will settleas it cools a bit. Before serving, let the potatoes cool until they're very warm but not hot (at least fifteen minutes), or serve them at room temperature.

Spinach Gratiné
(Epinard Gratiné)

Ingredients

- 1 (10oz.) bag fresh spinach
- Cooking spray
- 2/3 c. chopped onion
- 1/4 c. tub-style light cream cheese
- 1/2 tsp. dried oregano
- 1/4 tsp. salt
- 1/4 tsp. pepper
- 1 c. (1/4-inch-thick) sliced tomato
- 1/4 c. dry breadcrumbs
- 2 Tbsp. finely grated fresh Parmesan cheese

Instructions

1. Preheat oven to 375°F.
2. Remove large stems from spinach. Tear spinach into one-inch pieces; place in a colander. Rinse spinach under cold water; drain. Set aside.
3. Place a large dutch oven coated with cooking spray over medium heat until hot. Add onion; sauté for three minutes. Add spinach; cover and cook for two minutes or until spinach wilts. Add cream cheese, oregano, salt, and pepper. Uncover and cook for an additional minute or until cream cheese melts. Spoon spinach mixture into a one-quart gratin dish or shallow casserole dish coated with cooking spray. Arrange tomato slices in a single layer on top of spinach and sprinkle with breadcrumbs and Parmesan cheese. Bake at 375° for thirty minutes or until golden brown.

Spaghetti

Ingredients

- o 1 lb. spaghetti
- o 3 Tbsp. olive oil
- o 3 Tbsp. tomato paste
- o 1 Tbsp. garlic
- o 1 c. white onion
- o 1 tsp. fresh thyme, chopped
- o 4–5 chicken sausage, fish, hot dogs, or any other types of links or meat (organic meat preferably)
- o Salt and pepper to taste
- o 1 1/2 c. reserved pasta water

Instructions

Boil pasta according to package. In a heavy large saucepan, heat oil and add tomato sauce or ketchup (if using ketchup, add one additional tablespoon). Cook tomato paste for three to four minutes while stirring occasionally. Add garlic, onion, thyme, and cook for four minutes while stirring to blend. Add chicken bouillon and stir.

Add pasta, and stir to blend while gradually adding the pasta water. Lower heat and cover and cook for another four to five minutes. If desired, add crushed red pepper. Season with salt and pepper to taste. Serve hot.

SOUP DU JOUR

Callaloo Gumbo

Ingredients

- 2 lb. fresh crabmeat
- 3 Tbsp. peanut oil
- 3 scallions, including the green tops, minced
- 2 cloves garlic, minced
- 2 branches fresh thyme, crumbled, or 1/2 tsp. dried
- 1/2 lb. slab bacon, cut into 1/4-inch dice
- 1 lb. fresh spinach or callaloo greens, cleaned with stems removed
- 1 lb. okra, topped, tailed, and cut into rounds
- 7 c. water
- Salt and freshly ground black pepper
- 1 scotch bonnet–type chili, pricked with a fork
- Juice of 3 limes

Instructions

1. Brown the crabmeat in the oil with the scallions, one teaspoon of the garlic, and the crumbled thyme.
2. In a stockpot, brown the diced bacon.
3. Wilt the spinach in the rendered bacon fat.
4. Add the okra, cover with the water, and add salt and freshly ground black pepper to taste.
5. Cook for twenty minutes, stirring constantly with a whisk.
6. When done, add the crabmeat, remaining garlic, and chili that have been pricked with a fork.
7. Continue to cook over low heat for twenty minutes, stirring occasionally.
8. When done, add the lime juice, whisk it through thoroughly, and serve hot.

Try: Turkey / Chicken Bacon . not pork bacon.
Cabbage or lettuce instead of callaloo
Imitation Crab = pollock!

Haitian Bouillon
(Bouillon à l'Haitienne)

Ingredients

- 1 lb. meat, cubed beef or chicken
- 2 Tbsp. seasoned salt
- 2 limes, cut in half
- 2 sweet potatoes
- 1 boniata
- 1 spinach
- 2 potatoes
- 1 malanga
- 1 green pepper, sliced
- 3 carrots
- 2 onions, sliced
- 1 tsp. thyme
- 1 tsp. parsley
- 1/4 c. scallions
- 3 Tbsp. tomato paste
- Salt, black pepper, and hot pepper to taste

Instructions

1. Clean the meat with hot water and lemon.
2. Add seasoning salt, and set aside for two hours in a bowl. Combine meat and spinach in a stockpot with two quarts of water until meat is tender.
3. Add remaining ingredients, and cook for additional twenty minutes or until potatoes are cooked.

Squash Soup
(Soupe à la courge)

Ingredients

- 1 lb. cubed beef stew meat
- 1 lb. chicken
- 1 frozen squash (pumpkin or winter squash)
- 1 boniata
- 1 spinach
- 1 malanga
- 2 onions, sliced
- 3 large carrots
- 6 medium potatoes
- 1/4 lb. spaghetti or noodles
- 3 Tbsp. seasoned salt
- 2 limes, cut in half
- 2 tsp. thyme
- 2 tsp. parsley
- 1/2 c. scallions
- Salt, black pepper, and hot pepper to taste

Instructions

1. Clean the meat with hot water and lemon and set aside in a bowl.
2. Add seasoning salt, and set aside for two hours. Boil meat in stockpot with three quarts of water until tender (about 1 1/2–2 hours).
3. Add more additional water if necessary and remaining ingredients, except noodles. Cook for twenty minutes, and add noodles.

Chicken Broth Soup
(Bouillon de soupe au poulet)

It's a cure for any illness and the most important broth in your culinary repertoire. Early on in the cooking game, my mother, Berta, taught me how to make her chicken broth: not too much water, plenty of chicken pieces, parsnips for sweetness, skins left on the veggies for color, no strong boiling for clarity, and deflating for purity and health. Make ahead of time to store in the freezer so you'll always have some on hand.

Makes about four quarts.

Ingredients

- 6 lb. chicken backs and wings
- 4 ribs celery with leaves
- 4 carrots, unpeeled and halved
- 2 onions, unpeeled and halved
- 2 parsnips, unpeeled and halved
- 1 large ripe tomato or 3 ripe plum tomatoes, halved
- 4 cloves garlic, unpeeled and lightly bruised
- 8 sprigs fresh flat-leaf parsley, stems lightly bruised
- 4 sprigs fresh dill, stems lightly bruised (optional)
- 1 large bunch fresh thyme
- 6 black peppercorns
- 4 whole cloves
- 1 bay leaf
- 1 Tbsp. coarse salt or to taste
- 4 qt. water

Instructions

1. Rinse the chicken pieces well, removing all excess fat. Place the chicken in a large soup pot, and add all the remaining ingredients.
2. Bring to a boil over medium-high heat. Reduce the heat to medium, and simmer gently partially covered for 1 1/2 hours, carefully skimming off any foam that rises to the surface. Adjust the seasonings and cook for thirty minutes longer. Remove the pot from the heat, and let the broth cool slightly.

SALADS

Kidney Bean Salad
(Salade de haricot)

Whether served as a foil to a heavy entrée or as a light meal on their own, salads pull together the best of the season into a tasty mélange of fresh ingredients usually bound by a tangy dressing or sauce.

Ingredients

- 3 c. cooked kidney beans
- 2 onions (or chives), chopped
- 1/3 c. mayonnaise
- 1/2 cucumber, sliced
- 1/2 tsp. strong mustard
- 3/4 c. celery, chopped
- 1/2 tsp. each salt and pepper
- 4 hard-boiled eggs

Instructions

1. Mix all ingredients except for kidney beans and hard-boiled eggs with mayonnaise.
2. Then when mixed well, add beans and eggs.
3. Mix well.
4. Cover, and chill overnight.

French-Style Lettuce Salad
(Salade de laitue de style français)

Ingredients

- Head lettuce
- 1/4 tsp. salt
- 1 clove of garlic, sliced
- Freshly ground pepper
- 2 tbsp. olive oil
- 1 Tbsp. minced parsley
- 1 Tbsp. wine vinegar
- 1 tsp. lime juice

Instructions

1. Wash, drain, and thoroughly dry the lettuce.
2. Rub a salad bowl with garlic, and add the other ingredients to the bowl.
3. Mix well with salad spoon.
4. Crisscross salad fork and spoon in salad bowl to keep lettuce from dressing until ready to serve.
5. With hands, tear lettuce leaves and place over top of salad fork and spoon.
6. Just before serving, toss thoroughly.

Ratatouille

Ingredients

- 3 potatoes
- 1 large eggplant
- 3 zucchini
- 3 carrots
- 2 onions
- 2 green peppers
- 4 peeled tomatoes
- 2 Tbsp. tomato paste
- 3 Tbsp. lemon juice
- Dash of cinnamon
- 1/2 lb. meat cut into cubes (or meat balls)

Instructions

1. Fry all ingredients in a small amount of oil for one or two minutes.
2. In a saucepan, put one layer of vegetables, sprinkle with meat, and then another layer of vegetables.
3. Season with salt, pepper, and a little bit of cinnamon.
4. Mix tomato sauce with water and lemon juice.
5. Almost cover the vegetables with the sauce and let simmer until very little liquid is left.
6. Don't stir. Serve with white rice.

Haitian Coleslaw
(Salade de chou à l' Haïtienne)

Ingredients

- 1/4 c. mayonnaise
- 1/4 c. olive oil
- 1/4 c. fresh lime juice
- 2 Tbsp. apple cider vinegar
- 2 Tbsp. Dijon mustard
- 2 Tbsp. chopped fresh dill
- 1 Tbsp. sugar
- 2 small serrano chilies, seeded and minced (about 2 1/2 tsp.)
- 1 garlic clove, minced
- 1 tsp. celery seeds
- 8 c. (packed) shredded cabbage (about 1 1/4 lbs.)
- 2 c. (packed) shredded carrots (about 2 large)

Instructions

1. Whisk mayonnaise, olive oil, lime juice, apple cider vinegar, mustard, chopped dill, sugar, chilies, garlic, and celery seeds in medium bowl to blend.
2. Toss cabbage and carrots in a large bowl with enough dressing to coat.
3. Season to taste with salt and pepper.
4. Coleslaw can be prepared ahead.
5. Let stand at room temperature up to one hour or cover and refrigerate up to four hours.
6. Serve cold or at room temperature.

Haitian Fruit Salad

Ingredients

- 2 oranges
- 4 slices pineapple, diced
- 3 bananas
- 1/2 c. raspberries
- 1/2 c. melon balls
- 24 roasted nuts
- 1/2 c. strawberries
- 1/4 c. pineapple juice
- 1/4 c. lime juice
- 1 c. sweetened condensed milk beaten with 2 eggs

Instructions

1. Combine all ingredients. Mix the following ingredients together and pour over the fruit: pineapple juice, lime juice, and sweetened condensed milk beaten with two eggs.
2. Top with grated coconut (optional).

Haitian Potato Salad
(Salad de Pomme de Terre à l'Haitienne)

Charlene Chan of Chichilicious (ChichiLicious.com)

Ingredients

- 4 potatoes, peeled and cubed
- 1 carrot, peeled and minced
- 2 1/4 tsp. salt
- 1 small beet
- 2 eggs
- 1/2 c. sweet peas
- 1/2 onion, minced
- 1/3 c. red bell pepper, diced
- 1/3 c. red bell pepper, diced
- 2 tsp. mayonnaise
- 1/4 tsp. black pepper

Instructions

1. Boil potatoes and carrot in water with one teaspoon salt for ten minutes or until tender.
2. Boil beet separately in water with one teaspoon salt until tender, then peel and mince. Boil eggs separately in water with one-fourth teaspoon salt until hard.
3. In a bowl, place cubed potatoes, minced beet, sweet peas, carrots, onion, red and green bell peppers and mix with mayonnaise. Add black pepper.

Soveyo Salad

Ingredients

- 1/4 c. fresh lime juice
- 2 Tbsp. honey
- 1 Tbsp. redwine vinegar
- 1 tsp. minced garlic
- 1/4 c. olive oil, salt, and freshly ground black pepper
- 2 c. cubed mango, frozen/defrosted or jarred
- Head romaine (about 1 1/2pounds), chopped
- 1/2 seedless cucumber, cubed

Instructions

1. Whisk together juice, honey, vinegar, and garlic. Add oil in a slow stream, whisking until emulsified. Season with salt and pepper.
2. Toss together mangoes, romaine, and cucumber with dressing to taste.

Mountain Salad
(Salad de montagne)

Ingredients

- 3 hard-boiled eggs
- 1 mirliton
- 2 large carrots
- 1 c. peas
- 2 large potatoes
- 1 c. string beans
- 1/2 c. bean sprouts
- 2 medium beets
- 2 Tbsp. chopped celery leaves
- 2 Tbsp. chopped parsley
- 3 Tbsp. mayonnaise
- 1 small turnip
- 1 Tbsp. vinegar
- 1 small zucchini

Instructions

1. Boil and peel mirliton, carrots, potatoes, beets, turnip, and zucchini.
2. Boil peas and string beans.
3. Cut cooked vegetables into 1/2 inch cubes, cube eggs, and add peas and string beans.
4. Mix with parsley, celery leaves, mayonnaise, and vinegar.
5. Add salt and pepper to taste.

Russian Salad
(Salad Russe)

Ingredients

- 1 can (15 oz.) corn
- 1 lb. cooked green peas
- 1 lb. cooked green beans or 1 can French-style cut green beans
- 1 lb. carrots, peeled, cooked, and diced
- 1 lb. cooked beets, diced

Vinaigrette

- 1/4 c. chopped onions
- 1/4 c. chopped parsley
- Ground pepper to taste
- 1/3 c. white vinegar
- 1/2 c. olive oil
- Salt to taste

In Europe, especially Spain, it is more common to use mayonnaise, not vinaigrettes. The dressing in recipes is like this:

- 2 whole eggs or 2 yolks and 1 egg
- 1 c. olive oil
- Salt and pepper to taste
- Dash of lemon juice or vinegar (optional)

Instructions

1. Lightly whisk eggs, adding oil a drop at a time, increasing to a steady stream as mixture emulsifies. Add salt, pepper, and lemon juice or vinegar to taste without breaking the emulsion.
2. Mix all salad ingredients together in a large bowl. Serve with vinaigrette and enjoy!

Pikliz
(Haitian Spicy Pickled Vegetables)

Every Haitian home has a jar of *pikliz* on hand; it is a cultural classic. Cabbage, carrots, chilies, and other vegetables are soaked in vinegar to make a relish similar to American chowchow or Italian *giardiniera*. The crunchy salad is served as a side dish at Haitian meals. Flavored vinegar from *pikliz* is often used in marinades or to give dishes a spicy-sour punch.

Charlene Chan of Chichilicious (ChichiLicious.com)

Ingredients

- 6 scotch bonnet peppers
- 2 c. thinly sliced or shredded cabbage
- 1/2 c. thinly sliced or shredded carrots
- 1/4 c. thinly sliced or shredded onions
- 4 whole cloves
- 1 tsp. salt
- 8 to 10 peppercorns (optional)
- 3 c. vinegar

Instructions

1. Snip off the stem of the peppers, cut each into four pieces, and keep the seeds. Place hot peppers, cabbage, carrots, onion, cloves, salt, and peppercorn in a quart-size jar. Then add vinegar.
2. Close jar tightly and let sit at least twenty-four to forty-eight hours before serving.
3. Serve with meat or fish.

Pikliz with Garlic
(Pikliz à l'ail)

Ingredients

- 8 habanero peppers
- 4 Tbsp. of lime juice
- 2 c. of vinegar
- 1/2 onion, chopped
- 2 scallions, chopped
- 3 garlic cloves, chopped
- 2 c. of cabbage, shredded
- 2 c. of carrot, shredded
- 3 tsp. of sweet peas
- 2 whole shallots, chopped
- 2 fresh sprigs of thyme
- Pinch of salt
- Pinch of black pepper

Instructions

1. Combine all ingredients except vinegar into a mixing bowl and stir.
2. Pour into a large jar.
3. Add vinegar until filled to capacity.
4. Keep refrigerated and eat within three to five days for best flavoring.

Pikliz Puree

Ingredients

- 8 sprigs of thyme
- 1/4 red pepper
- 1/2 shallot, peeled
- 3 garlic cloves, peeled
- 1 scallion, chopped
- 3–4 sprigs of fresh parsley
- 1 Maggie chicken broth
- 1/2 scotch bonnet pepper
- 1/2 tsp. of black pepper
- 1/2 tsp. of adoboseasoning
- 1/2 c. of water
- 1/2 lemon, juiced

Instructions

1. Combine all ingredients in a blender.
2. Blend into a puree for two minutes.
3. Baste the freshly blended spices onto your choice of meat.
4. Let marinate overnight in the refrigerator.

THE SIDE SHOW

Cornmeal
(Mais Moulin Blanc)

Ingredients

- 1 c. cornmeal
- 4 c. water
- 1 minced garlic clove
- 1/2 finely chopped onion
- 1 tsp. thyme
- 1 tsp. parsley
- 1 Tbsp. oil
- Salt, black pepper, and hot pepper to taste

Instructions

1. Sauté garlic and onion in oil.
2. Add water and bring to a boil in a medium pot. Sauté garlic and onion in oil.
3. Combine remaining ingredients.
4. Stir mixture repeatedly to avoid clumps.

Fried Plantain
(Banan Péz é)

Charlene Chan of Chichilicious (ChichiLicious.com)

Haitian fried green plantains are a favorite snack and side dish in Haiti, Puerto Rico, Cuba, and the Dominican Republic. Haitians call them *banan pézé*. They are also eaten in Central America and throughout South America. In Ecuador, Peru, and Venezuela, they are known as *patacones*.

Ingredients

- 2 green plantains, peeled and sliced diagonally into 1-inch pieces
- Oil for deep frying

Method

1. Heat about one-half inch of oil in a heavy skillet over medium-high heat. Add half the plantain slices to the hot oil and fry, turning frequently until they begin to brown on all sides. Remove to a paper-towel-lined plate, and repeat with the remaining slices.
2. When all the slices have been fried, use a glass or small plate to press each slice to a thickness of about one-third inch.
3. Return half the flattened slices to the hot oil and fry again on each side until well browned and crispy. Drain on paper towels and repeat with the remaining flattened slices. Serve hot with *mojo* garlic sauce.

Variations

Sometimes the plantains are soaked in salted water for about an hour and then dried well before sautéing. This is said to make them crispier and add flavor.

Notes

In Haiti, *banan pézé* are usually served with *pikliz* and *griots* (fried pork). A *pézé* is a small device that is used in the Caribbean to flatten the plantains for their second frying. Any sturdy flat surface works just as well. Or try using a tortilla press. Use only green unripe plantains for this dish. They have higher starch content and will get crispier in the hot oil.

Rice with Black Mushrooms
(Diri Jon Jon)

Charlene Chan of Chichilicious (ChichiLicious.com)

Ingredients

- 2 c. of long-grain rice
- 1 c. dried black mushrooms
- 4 c. of water
- 2 chopped cloves of garlic
- 1 small onion, finely chopped
- 1 Tbsp. of oil
- Salt and pepper to taste

Instructions

1. Soak mushrooms in water overnight in a bowl.
2. Heat oil and fry onions and garlic cloves in a medium pot.
3. Discard mushrooms, and mix the water with onions and garlic. Add rice when water comes to a boil and simmer when it has dried.

Rice with Red Beans
(Riz et PoisCollée)

Ingredients

- 2 c. of long-grain rice
- 1 c. of red kidney beans
- 1 finely chopped onion
- 1 chopped hot green pepper
- 1/4 c. salt pork or bacon, cut into small cubes
- 1 Tbsp. of butter
- 2 chopped cloves of garlic
- 2 Tbsp. of vegetable oil
- Salt and pepper to taste

Instructions

1. Cook the beans in four cups of water for two hours or until tender in a medium pot.
2. Drain the beans, but keep the water, which will be used to cook the rice.
3. Fry the salt pork or bacon until crisp (use oil if needed). Add the onion, garlic, and green pepper.
4. Add the beans along with salt and pepper to taste. Add the water used to cook the beans and bring to a boil.
5. Add the rice and cook for twenty to twenty-five minutes.

SAUCES

Sauce Ti Malice

Charlene Chan of Chichilicious (ChichiLicious.com)

Ingredients

- 2 tsp. hot pepper
- 1 large chopped onion
- 1/2 c. chopped shallots or scallions
- 3 minced cloves of garlic
- 1/2 c. lemon or lime juice
- 1/4 c. oil
- Salt and pepper to taste

Instructions

1. Marinate onions with the lemon juice for two hours.
2. Combine all ingredients and boil in a pot for ten minutes until hot peppers are tender.
3. Allow to cool and store in a glass jar or bowl in the refrigerator.

Red Beans Sauce

(Sauce Pois Rouge)

Ingredients

- 2 c. dried red beans, rinsed
- 3 scallions
- 1 Tbsp. parsley
- 2 shallots
- 2 qt. water
- 1 c. cubed ham
- 2 chopped cloves of garlic
- Salt, black, and hot pepper to taste

Instructions

1. Combine scallions, parsley, shallots, and hot peppers to form a paste.
2. Heat oil on medium heat, and add seasoning paste, beans, and scallions. Add water, ham hock, parsley, and cubed ham and bring to boiling.
3. Cover and simmer for two hours or until beans are tender. Remove ham hock. Process beans and juice in an electric blender or force through a strainer.
4. Return sauce to low heat and season to taste.

Tomato Sauce

Ingredients

- 1 c. of water
- 1 1/2 Tbsp. tomato paste
- 1 small onion, sliced
- 1 garlic clove
- 1/4 c. red or green peppers
- 1 tsp. of oil
- Salt, black pepper, or hot pepper to taste

Instructions

1. Sauté onions and peppers in a pan for one minute.
2. Bring water to a boil, and add the remaining ingredients.
3. Stir and simmer sauce on low heat.
4. Serve with your favorite meat and rice.

Tchaka

Ingredients

- 1 c. each of
  pinto beans
  kidney beans
  small red beans
  dark red beans
- 2 c. dry corn (makes 8 cups)
- 1–2 lbs. beef, chicken, or pork cut into cubes
- Water
- 3 cloves garlic, minced
- 2 Tbsp. coconut milk
- 1 Tbsp. butter
- 3 Tbsp. parsley
- 2 chicken bouillon cubes
- 1 Tbsp. salt
- 1 scotch bonnet pepper

Instructions

1. If your beans are canned, rinse them and put them aside.
2. Mince or blend one clove of garlic, one tablespoon of parsley, one teaspoon of salt, and half a scotch bonnet pepper. Rub the beef with the spices and boil until tender.
3. Bring your water to a boil, add the salt, butter and garlic, and add the dry corn. It may take about two hours for the corn to be ready, but it will take shape when ready.
4. Add more water as it dissipates.
5. When your corn has been boiling for about 1 1/2 hours, add the beans and the beef, the coconut milk, the other half of the pepper, the remaining parsley, and the bouillon powder.

IN THE BREAD BASKET

Zucchini Bread
(Pain courgettes)

Ingredients

- 4 c. flour
- 3 eggs
- 1/2 tsp. salt
- 1 c. oil
- 1/4 tsp. baking powder
- 3 tsp. vanilla
- 1 tsp. baking soda
- 2 c. brown sugar
- 2 tsp. cinnamon
- 3 c. zucchini, grated
- 1 Tbsp. ground cloves

Instructions

1. Sift first six ingredients together.
2. Beat eggs and add to the remaining ingredients.
3. Mix flour mixture with zucchini mixture and pour into greased loaf pans.
4. Bake at 350°F degrees for one hour.

Raisin Bread
(Pain Raisin)

Ingredients

- 1/2 c. sugar
- 3 c. warm water
- 1 Tbsp. salt
- 2 Tbsp. yeast
- 3 Tbsp. shortening
- 5–6 c. flour
- 1 egg
- 1/2 c. raisins

Instructions

1. Dissolve yeast into one-half cup warm water.
2. Let stand in a warm place for about ten minutes.
3. Beat in the sugar, salt, shortening, egg, raisins, and the rest of the water.
4. Sift the flour and begin mixing it into the rest of the ingredients.

5. Knead, shape, and allow bread mixture to rise in oiled bowl until it has doubled in size.
6. Punch down and allow mixture to rise again in the baking pan.
7. To bake, place loaf in a cold oven.
8. Turn the heat to 400°F.
9. After fifteen minutes, reduce heat to 375°F degrees and bake for twenty-five minutes more.
10. Remove the loaf at once from the pan and cool on a rack before storing.

Corn Bread

(Pain de maïs)

Ingredients

- 2 Tbsp. melted butter
- 1/2 tsp. salt
- 1 c. flour
- 3 tsp. baking powder
- 3/4 c. corn meal
- 1 egg
- 1 1/2 Tbsp. sugar

Instructions

1. In a shallow pan about ten-by-fourteen-inch, melt butter.
2. Sift flour, corn meal, sugar, salt, and baking powder together into a large bowl.
3. Beat egg in smaller bowl, add milk, then melted butter, and gradually pour mixture into dry ingredients, mixing without beating until well blended.
4. Add a little more butter to pan, which should still be hot.
5. Pour in batter and bake twenty-five to thirty minutes in hot oven (425°F degrees).

Croissants

Ingredients

- 7/8 c. milk
- 1 cake yeast
- 1 Tbsp. lard
- 1/3 c. lukewarm water
- 1 1/2 tbsp. sugar
- 2 1/2 c. flour, sifted
- 3/4 tsp. salt
- 1 c. butter, softened

Instructions

1. Scald milk; add lard, sugar, and salt. Cool until lukewarm. Dissolve yeast in water then add to milk mixture. Stir in or knead in flour to make a soft dough.
2. Knead dough on a lightly floured surface until smooth and elastic. Place in a greased bowl and turn so all sides are lightly greased. Cover with a damp cloth. Let rise until doubled in bulk, about 1 1/2 hours. Cover the dough with a lid and chill thoroughly for at least twenty minutes.
3. Roll dough out into an oblong one-fourth inch thick.
4. Beat butter until creamy. Dot two-thirds of the surface of the dough with one-fourth cup of the butter. Fold the undotted third over the center third. Then fold the doubled portion over the remaining third of the butter-dotted portion. The dough is now three layers thick. Turn the layered dough a one-fourth turn and repeat. Do this two more times, making it a total of four times that you roll it and fold it. Cover and chill for at least two hours. Then roll the dough again on a floured surface. Cut the dough into three-inch squares. Cut the squares in half diagonally. Roll the triangular pieces, beginning with the wide side and stretching it slightly as you roll. Shape the rolls into crescents. Place on a baking sheet and chill for one-half hour. Preheat oven to 400°F degrees and bake for ten minutes, then reduce the heat to 350°F degrees and bake them for about ten to fifteen minutes longer or until done.

Recipe by Lucson Maddeus.

Haitian Brioche

Ingredients

- 1 pkg. active dry yeast
- 3 1/2 c. flour
- 1/2 c. butter
- 1/2 c. milk
- 1/3 c. sugar
- 4 eggs
- 1/2 tsp. salt
- 1 Tbsp. sugar

Instructions

1. Soften yeast in one-fourth cup warm water (110°F). Thoroughly cream butter, one-third cup sugar, and salt. Add one cup of flour and the milk to creamed mixture. Beat three eggs and one egg yolk together (reserve egg white). Add softened yeast and eggs to creamed mixture; beat well. Add remaining flour. By hand, beat for five to eight minutes. Cover; let rise in warm

place until doubled (about two hours). Stir down; beat well. Cover and refrigerate overnight.

2. Stir down; turn out on floured surface. Set aside one-fourth of dough. Cut remaining dough into six pieces as you would cut a pie; form each into four balls. With floured hands, tuck undercut edges. Place in greased muffin pans. Cut reserved dough in four wedges; divide each into six pieces; shape into twenty-four balls.

3. Make indentation in each large ball. Brush holes with water; press small balls into indentations. Cover; let rise until doubled (about thirty minutes). Combine one slightly beaten egg white and one tablespoon sugar; brush tops. Bake at 375°F for about fifteen minutes.

Homemade French Bread
(Ingredients de Pain Français)

Ingredients

- 2 pkg. dry yeast
- 2 c. boiling water
- 1/2 c. warm water
- 7 1/2–8 c. flour
- 2 Tbsp. sugar
- 1 egg, beaten
- 2 tsp. salt
- 2 Tbsp. milk
- 2 Tbsp. shortening
- Poppy or sesame seeds

Instructions

1. Dissolve yeast in warm water.
2. Combine sugar, shortening, salt, and water together and let cool to lukewarm.
3. Add in yeast mixture.
4. Stir in flour.
5. Knead for ten minutes or until smooth and elastic.
6. Place in greased bowl, turning once.
7. Let rise until doubled. Punch down and let rest for fifteen minutes. Divide dough in half.
8. On floured surface, roll each half to a twelve-by-fifteen-inch rectangle. Roll up starting at fifteen-inch edge.
9. Place loaves on greased cookie sheets and make four or five slashes diagonally across tops.
10. Let rise until doubled.
11. Mix egg and milk and brush on top of bread.
12. Sprinkle on poppy or sesame seeds if desired.
13. Bake at 400°F for twenty minutes.

THE SWEET LIFE: DESSERTS

Many types of desserts are eaten in Haiti, ranging from the mild to sweet. Sugarcane is used frequently in the making of these desserts; however, granulated sugar is also used often. One very popular dessert is *fresco*, which can be whipped up in no time. Fresco is similar to an Italian ice; however, it consists primarily of fruit syrup. The syrup is moderately thick and very sweet. It is frequently sold by street vendors. The sweet smell of this candy-like snack often attracts honeybees, and a common sight on the streets is a hurried vendor handing out frescos surrounded by swirls of bees. *Pain patate* is a soft sweetbread made using cinnamon, evaporated milk, and sweet potato. It is usually served cold from the refrigerator, but it can be eaten at room temperature. *Akasan* is a thick corn milkshake with a consistency similar to that of *labouille* (in Creole, "labouyi," a popular porridge made from corn). It is made using many of the same ingredients as *pain patate*, consisting of evaporated milk, sugar, and corn flour.

Fried Bananas
(Beyen)

Ingredients

- 3 very ripe bananas
- 1 Tbsp. flour
- 1/2 tsp. cinnamon powder
- 1/2 tsp. vanilla extract
- 1 Tbsp. sugar
- 1/8 tsp. baking soda
- Sugar for topping (optional)

Instructions

1. Mix bananas, flour, sugar, vanilla, and cinnamon in a medium-size bowl.
2. Place spoonful of batter in very hot oil and fry until golden brown. Sprinkle with sugar.

Potato Pie

(Pain Patate)

Pain patate is Haiti's sweet potato pudding. A rich, delectable dessert that is the perfect finishing touch.

Ingredients

- 2 1/2 lbs. bonito (white sweet potato)
- 4 ripe bananas, mashed
- 1/2 c. shortening
- 1 can cream of coconut
- 1 (8 oz.) can coconut or evaporated milk
- 4 Tbsp. butter or margarine
- 3/4 c. brown sugar
- 1 Tbsp. ground ginger
- 1/2 Tbsp. vanilla extract
- 1 Tbsp. ground cinnamon
- 1 tsp. ground nutmeg
- 1/2 tsp. salt
- 1 c. raisins

Instructions

Preheat oven to 350°F (176°C). Wash and peel bonitos (*patates*) and cut into small pieces. Finely grind bonitos (*patates*) with the coconut milk using a food processor. Place in a heavy eight- to-ten-quart dutch oven. Peel and finely blend bananas. Add banana mixture and mix well. Then add all remaining ingredients (except for raisins) and mix well. Cook on medium heat, stirring constantly with wooden spoon until brown (about thirty-five to forty minutes). Simmer for about five minutes on low heat. Remove from heat, add raisins, and mix well. Pour the mixture into a fifteen-inch oven-safe dish. Bake for thirty-five minutes or until golden brown. Sprinkle with sugar and let sit for half an hour before serving.

Haitian Pound Cake

(Gâteau à l'Haïtienne)

Ingredients

- 2 sticks of butter
- 2 c. of flour
- 1 c. of sugar
- 5 eggs, at room temperature
- 1 tsp. baking powder
- Pinch of salt
- 1 Tbsp. of vanilla extract
- 3/4 c. milk (boil a cup of milk with several sticks of cinnamon and let reduce to 3/4 c., and let cool and discard the cinnamon sticks)

several cinnamon sticks

Try coconut milk

Instructions

1. Preheat the oven to 325°F. Grease two 8 1/2 round pans.
2. In an electric mixer, cream the butter and sugar. Mix until the mixture is light, fluffy, and smooth. Add the eggs one at a time, beating well after each egg.

3. In a mixing bowl, combine the remaining two cups of flour, baking powder, and salt. With the machine running, add one-fourth cup of the flour mixture at a time, gradually adding milk. Mix well. Pour the filling into the prepared pan.
4. Bake for about fifty minutes or until the center is firm. Remove from the oven and cool on a wire rack for thirty minutes. Use any flavor of icing.

Rhum Barbancourt Crème Brûlée
(Spiced Rum Crème Brûlée)

This dessert is a classic French custard infused with Haitian rum, giving it a refreshing twist. This extravagantly rich brûlée will melt on your tongue, bursting with flavor, and is sure to be a hit at any gathering. Rhum Barbancourt is a delicious spiced rum with a flavor reminiscent of citrus. Made locally in Haiti using sugarcane instead of molasses, it is a national favorite and can be found in most groceries and liquor stores. The secret to a great brûlée is lower heat with longer cooking time, so take your time and have fun!

Serves six.

Ingredients

- 2 1/2 c. heavy cream
- 1/3 c. sugar
- 6 egg yolks
- 3 Tbsp. Rhum Barbancourt
- 1/4 c. sugar to finish
- Fresh raspberries

Instructions

1. Pour heavy cream in a saucepan on high heat and remove from heat just before boiling.
2. In a mixing bowl, separate egg yolks, stir in sugar with a fork, and then add the rum.
3. Slowly pour the cream into the egg yolks while stirring the whole time. Adding too much heat too quickly will cook the egg yolks early. Use a mesh strainer to strain back into pan.
4. Place six oven ramekins into a roasting pan filled halfway up the ramekins with hot water. Ladle the custard into each ramekin. Bake in a preheated oven at 350°F degrees for twenty-five to thirty minutes until they have a slight softness at the center.
5. Let cool in water and then refrigerate for four hours to overnight; the longer they set, the firmer the custard. Sprinkle with sugar, and caramelize with a blowtorch before serving. Garnish with raspberries on top.

Rice Pudding Crème Brûlée
(Riz au Lait Crème Brûlée)

Serves six.

Ingredients

- 2 c. whole milk
- 1/2 c. risotto rice
- 1/4 c. sugar
- 4 egg yolks
- 1 c. heavy cream
- 1 tsp. vanilla extract
- 1/4 c. fine sugar to finish

Directions

1. Pour the milk into a saucepan on high heat. As soon as it begins to boil, add rice and cook over medium to low heat for fifteen minutes, stirring occasionally to keep from overboiling until only one-third of the milk is remaining, and remove from heat.
2. Separate egg yolks into a bowl; add sugar, cream, and vanilla extract; and mix well. Slowly strain the egg yolk mixture into the rice while stirring so you do not heat the egg too quickly.
3. Place six oven ramekins in a roasting pan filled halfway up the ramekins with hot water. Spoon the rice-and-custard mixture into each ramekin and bake in a preheated oven at 350°F degrees for twenty to twenty-five minutes until the custard is slightly firm in the middle.
4. Leave the dishes to cool in the water for half an hour. Sprinkle with sugar, and caramelize the top with a blowtorch before serving.

Haitian Doughboys

(Doughboys haïtiens)

Ingredients

- 1 egg
- 1 c. flour
- 1/2 c. sugar
- Pinch of salt
- 3 bananas, puréed
- 1/2 c. water
- 1/4 tsp. each of vanilla, cinnamon, and nutmeg
- Oil for frying

Instructions

1. Combine flour, sugar, and salt in a medium-size bowl; stir.
2. Add remaining ingredients and mix well, forming a thin pancake-like batter (no baking powder or soda is used).
3. Heat two cups of vegetable oil in a deep skillet until very hot.
4. Pour one ladle full of batter into hot oil.
5. Fry on one side until golden brown.
6. Then turn and fry other side.
7. Drain on paper towel.
8. Sprinkle with granulated sugar, and eat warm.

This doughnut, like dessert, goes great with the Haitian fruit salad on page 81.

Blancmange

Blancmange is a creamy coconut custard with fruit cocktail, an ambrosial dessert that melts in your mouth. Originally a French dessert, it is generally served cold and, centuries ago, was also prepared in a savory fashion with shredded meat.

Serves four to eight.

Ingredients

- 1 (12 oz.) can coconut milk
- 2 (12 oz.) cans of evaporated milk
- 1 (12 oz.) can fruit cocktail
- 1 tsp. vanilla extract
- 1/2 tsp. cinnamon powder
- 3 pkgs. gelatin
- 1 in. lime zest
- Sugar to taste

Instructions

Dissolve the gelatin in three-fourths cup of boiled water. Place evaporated milk in a large saucepan. Add sugar to a taste then bring to a boil. Add cinnamon powder, vanilla extract, and lime zest to the mixture. Add the gelatin to milk mixture. Then add coconut milk and sugar to taste. Drain fruit cocktail and add to mixture. Mix well, and place in a large bowl or mold. Refrigerate for at least six hours prior to serving. Can be enjoyed directly out of serving dishes or removed from mold first if one is used.

Akasan "AK-100"

Ingredients

- 2 cinnamon sticks
- 4 to 6 anise star
- 1 c. very fine corn flour
- Dash of salt
- 1 tsp. vanilla extract
- 2 (12 oz.) cans evaporated milk
- Sugar to taste

Instructions

1. Boil four cups of water with cinnamon and anise stars. Dilute corn flour in one cup cold water with a dash of salt.
2. Slowly pour liquefied corn flour into boiling water, stirring constantly until it thickens but for no more than five minutes. Add vanilla extract and can of evaporated milk, and allow to completely cool.
3. Refrigerate if you like it cold. If you prefer it warm, add evaporated milk and sugar to taste as if making a cup of coffee.
4. Always remove anise star and cinnamon before serving. Serve with evaporated milk.

Plantain Puree

(Llabouyi Bannann)

Ingredient

- 1 green plantain
- 1 ripe banana
- 1 (12 oz.) can evaporated milk
- 1 (12 or 14 oz.) can coconut milk or 1 c. milk
- 1/4 tsp. vanilla extract
- 3 cinnamon sticks
- 2 whole anise stars
- Pinch of grated nutmeg
- 1/2 c. sugar (white or brown)
- 1/2 tsp. grated lime rind or 1/2 in. whole lime rind

Instructions

1. Peel the plantain. Cut into one-half-inch slices. In a blender, puree plantain pieces; add 2 cups water and ripe banana *or* grate the plantain, mash the banana, and mix both with two cups water to get a puree.
2. In a saucepan, add plantain puree and bring to a boil on low-medium heat.
3. Add evaporated milk, coconut milk, vanilla extract, anise stars, nutmeg, sugar, and lime rind.
4. Cook for fifteen to twenty minutes, stirring occasionally so that it does not stick to the bottom of the pot. Consistency should be like oatmeal.

Rice Pudding
(Riz au Lait)

Rice with milk is one of the most popular desserts in the Caribbean and the Latin world. This simple sweet conjures up memories of home and is a supreme comfort food.

Makes four to six servings.

Ingredients

- 4 c. milk
- 1/2 c. short-grain rice
- 1 cinnamon stick
- 1 orange or lemon, peeled
- Pinch of salt
- 1/4 c. raisins

- o 1/2 c. sugar
- o 2 Tbsp. butter
- o 1 tsp. vanilla

Instructions

1. Place the milk, rice, cinnamon stick, orange or lemon peel, and salt in a medium saucepan and bring to a boil over medium heat. Immediately reduce heat to very low and simmer, stirring often and scraping bottom for about forty-five minutes.
2. Add the raisins and sugar and simmer for another fifteen minutes. Stir often to keep from sticking to the bottom of the pot.
3. Remove from heat and stir in the butter and vanilla. Adjust sugar to taste and serve hot or cold, sprinkling the top with some ground cinnamon.

Variations

- o *Arroz con Dulce* (Puerto Rico) or *Arroz-Doce* (Brazil): use coconut milk in place of regular milk.
- o Short-grain rice, like arborio or Valencia rice, is best for rice pudding as it gives the dessert a creamier texture, but regular long-grain rice can be used to a good result too. A little more rice can be added if you want a firmer pudding. If the pudding gets too thick, just add a little more milk.
- o Sometimes water, cream, sweetened condensed milk, or evaporated milk is substituted for the regular milk. Just make sure the total amount of liquid adds up to four cups, and adjust the amount of sugar as needed.
- o Add one or two tablespoons of brandy or rum when you stir in the butter and vanilla if you like.
- o Some recipes call for stirring in two beaten egg yolks at the end before adding the butter and vanilla. The heat of the pudding will cook the yolks, make it creamier, and give it a pale golden color.

MANJE KREYÒL
HAITIAN CRÉOLE FOOD

"Manje Kreyòl" (Haitian Creole) is the equivalent of *criollo* cooking (*criollo* meaning "Creole") in other countries. This encompasses most of what is regularly cooked in Haiti, involving the extensive use of herbs and, somewhat unlike Cuban cooking, the liberal use of peppers. A typical dish would probably be a plate of *du riz colée a pois* (diri kole ak pwa), which is brown rice with red kidney or pinto beans glazed with a marinade as a sauce and topped off with red snapper, tomatoes, and onions. The dish can be accompanied by *bouillon* (bouyon), known as *sancocho* in some neighboring countries. Bouillon is a hearty stew consisting of various spices, potatoes, tomatoes, and meats such as goat or beef.

Rice is occasionally eaten with beans alone, but more often than not, some sort of meat completes the dish. Chicken (*poul*) is frequently eaten; the same goes for goat meat (*kabrit*) and beef (*bèf*). Chicken is often boiled in a marinade consisting of lemon juice, sour orange, scotch bonnet pepper, garlic, and other seasonings and subsequently fried until crispy.

Legume is a thick vegetable stew consisting of a mashed mixture of eggplant, cabbage, chayote, spinach, watercress, and other vegetables, depending on availability and the cook's preference. It is flavored with epis, onions, garlic, and tomato paste and generally cooked with beef and/or crab. *Legume* is most often served with rice but may also be served with other starches, including *mayi moulen* (a savory cornmeal porridge similar to polenta or grits), *pitimi* (cooked millet), or *ble* (wheat groats).

Other starches commonly eaten include yam, *patate* (neither of which should be confused with the North American sweet potato), potato, and breadfruit. These are frequently eaten with a thin sauce consisting of tomato paste, onions, spices, and dried fish.

Tchaka is a hearty stew consisting of hominy, beans, *joumou* (pumpkin), and meat (often pork). *Tchaka* is eaten by people and also used as an offering to the *Loa* in Voodoo.

Spaghetti is most often served in Haiti as a breakfast dish and is cooked with hot dog, dried herring, and spices and served with ketchup and sometimes raw watercress.

One of the country's best known appetizers is *paté*, which are meat or salted cod patties surrounded by a crispy or flaky crust. Other snacks include *akra* (crispy, spicy fried malanga fritters), *banann pese*, and *marinad* (fried savory dough balls). For a complete meal, they may be served with *griyo* (fried pork) or other fried meat. These foods are served with a spicy slaw called *pikliz*, which consists of cabbage, carrot, vinegar, scotch bonnet pepper, and spices. Fried foods, collectively known as *fritay*, are sold widely on the streets.

Regional dishes also exist throughout Haiti. In the area around Jérémie on Haiti's southwest tip, people eat a dish called *tom-tom*, which is steamed breadfruit (*lam veritable*) mashed in a *pilon* and is very similar to West African *fufu*. Tom-tom is swallowed without chewing using a slippery sauce made of okra (*kalalou* in Haitian Creole) cooked with meat, fish, crab, and savory spices. Another regional dish is *poul AK nwa* (chicken with cashew nuts), which is from the north of the country, in the area around Cap Haitian.

Waves of migration have also influenced Haitian cuisine. For example, immigrants from Lebanon and Syria brought kibble, which has been adopted into Haitian cuisine.

The flavor base of much Haitian cooking is epis, a combination sauce made from cooked peppers, garlic, and herbs—particularly green onions, thyme, and parsley. It is used as a basic condiment for rice and beans and is also used in stews and soups.

Increasingly, imported Maggi bouillon cubes are used by Haitian cooks. This is indicative of the growing availability of imported, often artificial and inexpensive foods, such as Tampico beverages.

NATIONAL SPIRITS AND LIQUORS

Beer

Beer is one of several common alcoholic beverages consumed in Haiti, often drunk at festivals, parties, and occasionally downed with a meal. The most widely drunk brand of beer in Haiti is Prestige, a nationally popular mild lager with a taste similar to many commercialized beers such as Budweiser and Miller Light. The beer has a light and crisp yet mildly sweet taste with a vague yet strong flavor reminiscent of several American-style beers. Prestige is brewed by Brasserie Nationale d'Haiti.

Rum

Haiti is home to one of the most well-known and world-renowned rum distilleries, Rhum Barbancourt. It is one of the nation's most famous exports and, by international standards, the country's most popular alcoholic beverage – popular amongst many as well as rum connoisseurs. It is unique in that the distilleries use sugarcane juice directly instead of molasses like other types of rum. The rum is marketed in approximately twenty countries and uses a process of distillation similar to the process used to produce cognac.

Crémas

The liquor-creamed drink called *crémas* is also a popular Haitian drink. It is a sweet and creamy alcoholic beverage usually consumed as part of dessert or simply by itself.

Ingredients

- 2 (12 oz) cans of evaporated milk
- 4 (12 oz) cans of sweetened condensed milk
- 1 (15 oz) can cream of coconut (not to be confused with coconut milk)
- 1 tsp. vanilla extract
- 1 tsp. almond extract
- 1 anise star
- 1 tsp. ground cinnamon
- 1 tsp. grated nutmeg
- 1 lime (zest and juice)
- 750 mL 80 proof rum

Instructions

1. Pour rum into a large pot.
2. Add the evaporated milk, sweetened condensed milk, and cream of coconut (warm up the cream of coconut prior to adding by running hot water over the can), and stir the ingredients together until well blended.
3. Mix in the remaining ingredients.
4. Let sit for 15 – 30 minutes, and then bottle and refrigerate.

Clairin

Clairin or *kleren* is another popular drink; it is equivalent to moonshine and is distilled from molasses. It is distilled twice sometimes to have a higher proof of alcohol. It is widely popular, and small distilleries can be found throughout the countryside. *Clairin* is at least 100 to 120 proof. Double distilled, it can easily be 150 to 190 proofs. *Clairin* may be more popular than rum because it is much cheaper and less labor intensive to make.

NONALCOHOLIC BEVERAGES

Juice is a mainstay in Haiti due to its tropical climate. Juices from many fruits are commonly made and can be found everywhere. Guava juice, grapefruit juice, mango juice, along with the juices of many citrus fruits (oranges, granadilla, passion fruit, etc.). Juice is the *de facto* beverage because of its variety of flavors, easy production, and widespread accessibility. Malta is also a popular nonalcoholic drink consisting of unfermented barley with molasses added for flavor. In more urban areas of the nation, the people enjoy Americanized drinks, such as an array of soft drinks in which Coca Cola dominates all other local soft drinks. Milkshakes are also enjoyed regularly.

Papaya Juice
(Jus Papaye)

Ingredients

- 1/2 papaya, peeled and diced
- Crushed ice
- 2 pinches of salt
- 1 can of evaporated milk
- 3 Tbsp. of sugar
- 1 tsp. of vanilla extract

Instructions

1. Put all the ingredients in a blender and blend on high.
2. Pour into glasses and enjoy!

INDEX

A

adobo seasoning salt, 29
AK-100. *See* akasan
anise stars, 146, 147
appetizers, 17, 19, 151
    baked kibbe, 36
    beef patties, 32
    corn fritters, 38
    fish fritters, 39
    mini quiches, 22
    onion tart, 27
    pimento cheese, 20
    taro root fritters, 25
At-Risk Children Foundation
    (ARCF), 7, 9, 11, 12, 13, 17
Aubergine au Parmesan. See
    eggplant Parmesan
avocados, 23
avocados stuffed with crabmeat, 23

B

bacon, 90, 119,
baked kibbe, 36
baking powder, 25, 26, 34, 35, 39,
    40, 41, 126, 129, 139, 140,
    144

Banan Pézé. See fried plantain
beef patties, 32
beef stew, 59, 93
beer, 153
Beignets de Conque. See conch
    fritters
Beignets de Maïs. See corn fritters
Beignets de Poisson. See fish fritters
Beignets de Poulet. See chicken
    fritters
Beyen. See fried bananas
blancmange, 145
bouillon, 150
Bouillon a l'Haitienne. See Haitian
    bouillon
Boulettes de Bœuf Assaisonné. See
    seasoned beef meatballs
Budweiser, 153

C

Canard Rôti Avec Sauce à L'orange.
    See roast duck with orange
    sauce
chicken broth soup, 95
chicken Creole, 50
chicken in sauce, 45
clairin, 155

corn fritters, 38
cornmeal, 16, 115, 151
Creole lobster, 68
Crevettes à la Créole. See shrimp
    Creole
criollo, 150

D

dessert
    akasan, 135, 146
    blancmange, 145
    potato pie, 137
    Rhum Barbancourt cremé
        brûlée, 141, 143
    rice pudding, 143, 148
Dinde en Sauce. See turkey in sauce
Diri Jon Jon. See rice with black
    mushrooms
du riz colée a pois, 150

E

eggplant mixed and watercress, 77
eggplant Parmesan, 79
entrée
    roast duck with orange sauce, 51
    roti chicken, 43
epis, 142

F

fish fritters, 39
frescos, 135
fried cubed beef or goat, 55

G

Galettes de Boeuf. See beef patties
Galettes de Poulet. See chicken
    patties

gratiné
    macaroni gratiné, 82
    potato gratiné, 84
grilled salmon, 72

H

Haitian bouillon, 91
Haitian potato salad, 103
Homard Creole. See Creole lobster

I

Italian ice, 135

J

juices, 44, 49, 52, 53, 56,
Jus Papaye. See papaya juice

K

kibble, 151
kidney bean salad, 98
kleren. See clairin

L

labouille, 135
Lambi en Sauce. See stewed conch
legume, 75, 76, 150
Llabouyi Bannann. See plantain
    puree

M

macaroni gratiné, 82
Maggi bouillon cubes, 151
Mais Moulin Blanc. See cornmeal
Malanga Acra Beignets. See taro root
    fritters

malta, 156
Manje Kreyòl, 150
marinated red snapper, 67
Miller Light, 153
moonshine, 155

O

onion tart, 27

P

Pain Patates. See potato pie
Pain Raisin. See raisin bread
pasta, spaghetti, 82, 87, 88
pastry, Hatian brioche, 132
paté, 9, 151
pikliz, 62, 110, 112, 113, 117, 151
pimento cheese, 20
plantain puree, 147
Poisson Cuit a la Vapeur. See
    steamed fish
Porc Frit Griots. See fried pork
    cubed
potato pie, 137
Poulet Créole. See chicken Creole
Poulet en Sauce. See chicken in
    sauce
Poulet Roti. See roti chicken
Prestige, 153

R

Ragoût de Boeuf. See beef stew
Ragoût de Légumes Mélangés. See
    mixed vegetable stew
red beans sauce, 122
red meat 54
    beef stew, 59, 93
    fried cubed beef or goat, 55
    seasoned beef meatballs, 57

Red Snapper Mariné. See marinated
    red snapper
Rhum Barbancourt crème brûlée,
    141
rice, 15, 16, 46, 50, 60, 70, 71, 76,
    78, 100, 118, 119, 123, 143,
    148, 149, 150, 151
rice pudding, 148, 149
rice pudding crème brûlée, 143
rice with black mushrooms, 118
rice with red beans, 119
Riz au Lait. See rice pudding
Riz au Lait Crème Brûlée. See rice
    pudding crème brûlée
roast duck with orange sauce, 51
roti chicken, 43
rum, 153
Russian salad, 108
Rz et Pois Collée. See rice with red
    beans

S

*Salad de Pomme de Terre a
    l'Haitienne. See* Haitian potato
    salad
Salad Russe. See Russian salad
salads
    Haitian potato salad, 103
    kidney bean salad, 98
    Russian salad, 108
    soveyo salads, 105
sancocho, 150
Sauce Pois Rouge. See red beans
    sauce
sauces
    red beans sauce, red beans sauce
    Tchaka, 124, 151
Saumon Grillé. See grilled salmon
seafood
    Creole lobster, 68

grilled salmon, 72
shrimp Creole, 70
side dish, 110, 116
  fried plantain, 61, 116
  rice with black mushrooms, 118
  rice with red beans, 119
soup du jour
  chicken broth soup, 95
  Haitian bouillon, 91
  squash soup, 87
Soup Joumou. See squash soup
spaghetti, 87, 93, 151
spiced rum crème brûlée. *See*
    Rhum Barbancourt crème
    brûlée
spinach gratiné, 86
squash soup, 93
steamed fish, 65
stewed conch, 64
sugarcane, 17, 135, 141, 153

T

Tarte a l'Oignon. See onion tart
Tassot au Bouef—Cabrit. See fried
    cubed beef or goat
Tchaka, 124, 151
tom-tom, 151
turkey in sauce, 47

V

vegetables, eggplant mixed and
    watercress, 77

achiote — annatto.
Boniata : Ja. Sweet Potato.
Malanga : Ja. Coco, Taro.
adobo : seasoning for marinating

Lightning Source UK Ltd.
Milton Keynes UK
UKOW04f2357171215

264916UK00001B/218/P